GILBERT

GILBERT

The Last Years of
W.G. Grace

Charlie Connelly

GILBERT

The Last Years of
W.G. Grace

Charlie Connelly

B L O O M S B U R Y

LONDON · NEW DELHI · NEW YORK · SYDNEY

John Wisden & Co Ltd
An imprint of Bloomsbury Publishing Plc

50 Bedford Square
London
WC1B 3DP
UK

1385 Broadway
New York
NY 10018
USA

www.bloomsbury.com

WISDEN and the wood-engraving device are trademarks of John Wisden
& Company Ltd, a subsidiary of Bloomsbury Publishing Plc

First published 2015

www.wisden.com
www.wisdenrecords.com
Follow Wisden on Twitter @WisdenAlmanack
and on Facebook at Wisden Sports

British Library Cataloguing-in-Publication Data
A catalogue record for this book is available from the British Library.

Library of Congress Cataloguing-in-Publication data has been applied for.

ISBN: HB: 978-1-4729-1758-4
ePub: 978-1-4729-1759-1

2 4 6 8 10 9 7 5 3 1

Typeset in 11pt Adobe Garamond Pro by Deanta Global Publishing Services,
Chennai, India
Printed and bound in Great Britain by CPI Group (UK) Ltd, Croydon CR0 4YY

To find out more about our authors and books visit www.wisden.com.
Here you will find extracts, author interviews, details of forthcoming events
and the option to sign up for our newsletters.

BY THE SAME AUTHOR

Monday 18 July 1898

He awoke, breathed deeply, rubbed one eye and didn't feel any different. The aches from Saturday's exertions – five Somerset wickets to add to the seven he'd taken in the first innings – had long subsided bar the soreness in his bruised heel, and any lingering shudders and vibrations from the previous evening's rail journey had seeped from his bones and into the mattress during the night.

He threw back the covers, swung his legs out of the bed, sat up, spat into the chamber pot, cleared each nostril in turn, smoothed his beard and sat still, allowing the last mists of sleep to disperse from his mind. Balling his fists against the edge of the mattress, he heaved himself to his feet, padded to the window and opened the curtains. The early morning light was pale gold from a near-white sky and the rays fell warmly on his face. It was going to be a beautiful day and the wicket would be fast.

He'd never set any great store by birthdays but was prepared to concede that this one might be different, at least from the outside. It's not every birthday that sees MCC move one of the iron horses of the fixture list in order to mark it (when told about it he'd joked that if it had to happen it was easier to move the match than his birthday). He didn't feel 50 years old, but then he wasn't entirely sure how being 50 years old was supposed to feel. He was playing with men who hadn't been born when he was already playing first-class cricket but he was still bowling them out and driving them to the boundary. Fifty to him was just a number worthy of a brief raising of the bat before facing the next ball. Besides, he was more enthused by leading the Gentlemen against the Players, always one of the highlights of his season, than anything else. The game was arguably the highlight of the domestic cricket calendar as well and he'd been such a constant presence since his first selection for the Gentlemen in 1865, two weeks before his seventeenth birthday, that it had become almost his own personal fixture.

By the time he reached Lord's at around eleven o'clock the ground was already almost full. Word of his arrival raced around the spectators and it was all he could do to reach the little mobile post office set up towards the nurseries and scoop up the heap of congratulatory telegrams that awaited him. The number of well-wishers meant he wouldn't have the opportunity for his customary knock-up in the nursery nets, and by the time he had negotiated his way slowly through the happy multitude to the Pavilion his jaw was already aching through constant smiling and his shoulders were warm from the congratulatory back slaps.

The Pavilion provided a little relief from the throng but still everyone lining the stairs and landings all the way to the dressing-room wanted to wish the Old Man many happy returns as he passed. While thoroughly enjoying the extraordinary wave of goodwill washing over him, it was with some relief that he was able to close the door behind him.

The rest of the team expressed their hearty congratulations, with one exception, but the antipathy at that stage was mutual.

As the Champion entered the room Charlie Kortright, the fearsome fast bowler from Essex, lifted his foot on to the bench and thumbed at the toe of his boot with stern concentration. Ordinarily he'd at least have shaken the veteran's hand but he was still angry.

Just over a week ago Gloucestershire had travelled to Leyton to play Essex and, aided by the Doctor's 126 in their first innings, were set 147 to win the match. Late on the second evening Grace played a ball back low towards the bowler, Walter Mead, who lunged forward and appealed for a caught and bowled. The umpire, George Burton, gave Grace out.

The batsman straightened and looked down the wicket, his face a picture of disbelief.

'Come now, George,' said Grace, his voice even more highly pitched than usual, 'the ball was clearly grounded first.'

'I think it carried, Doctor,' said the umpire, confirming his decision.

'Carried, George? *Carried?*' The volume of his voice rose at the same level as his anger. 'Why, a man at Leyton station could have seen the ball grounded. For goodness' sake, man, I'm not out.'

He stood his ground and glared at the umpire.

Burton swallowed.

'I think in the circumstances,' he said, 'there is sufficient doubt about the catch to permit the Doctor to continue.'

'Thank you, George,' said Grace, taking up his stance again. 'Mr Mead, you may continue, there is a match to be decided.'

The Essex men seethed, thinking back to an incident early the previous day when the Doctor had claimed a caught and bowled from Perrin when most people in the ground were convinced the ball had reached Grace on the bounce. He'd scooped the ball up, thrown it in the air and yelled, 'Not bad for an old 'un!' With a certain degree of hesitancy, up went the umpire's finger and Perrin had to go.

A handful of overs into the next morning's play, Kortright hurled down a thunderbolt that appeared to trap the Champion, needing one run for his half-century, plumb leg before. Grace stood up straight, bridling in the face of Kortright's appeal, and stared down the wicket. The umpire caught his gaze, looked away and said, very quietly, 'Not out.' Kortright was dumbfounded and stalked back to the end of his long run. The next ball was faster, just short of a length, broke slightly off the wicket, nicked the edge of the Doctor's bat and, with a roar of triumph from the bowler, was pouched by first slip. Again Grace stood erect and glared down the wicket. Somewhere among the applause came another halting 'not out' from the umpire, and when the bowler looked round there was the Doctor, studiously re-marking his guard with a bail.

Kortright retrieved the ball, stamped his way back to his mark, turned, and hurtled in to bowl what was, feasibly, a hat-trick ball against the man considered the greatest player in the game. He was already arguably the fastest bowler in the country but the ball he produced this time was quick even by his standards. It pitched on a length, fizzed past the Old Man's defence and knocked both leg and middle stumps clean out of the ground. The Champion tucked his bat under his arm and was taking his first steps towards the pavilion when the still furious bowler, drawing almost level with him in his follow-through, loudly proclaimed, 'Surely you're not leaving us, Doctor? There's one stump still standing!'

Grace paused briefly as if he were about to turn and respond, but instead marched off at a quickened pace, announcing to the waiting members as he strode up the steps that he had never been so insulted in his life, then bellowing his way through the pavilion to the dressing-room about this outrageous slight questioning his integrity and sportsmanship coming from a man who purported to be a gentleman. Even the longest-serving Gloucestershire players, who had heard many a verbal eruption from behind the famous beard, could not remember him ever being so angry.

And now here were the same two men, barely a week later, sharing a dressing-room. Not only that, Grace was the captain and Kortright his main strike bowler. Thank goodness, thought the other players, there was W.G.'s birthday to distract attention from the feud.

Just after midday Grace, having lost the toss, led the Gentlemen down the stairs and through the Long Room. He'd barely reached the doors to the members' seats when the roar of appreciative recognition from the crowd rumbled up like a train emerging from a tunnel. The members all stood with their faces turned to him and without a pause he passed between them and walked through the gate on to the field. The entire crowd was on its feet cheering and applauding, straw hats waving in the air like so many ears of corn.

Touched, faintly embarrassed and not wishing to detract from the solemnity of the match, yet feeling he should acknowledge this unprecedented ovation, he grinned and raised his right hand in a mock military salute as he strode across the outfield.

Reaching the wicket he set the field, took the ball from the umpire and threw it wordlessly to Kortright to open the bowling. Arthur Shrewsbury and Bobby Abel walked out to open the innings for the professionals with Shrewsbury taking guard for the first over. The Gentlemen's wicketkeeper Gregor MacGregor took a few strides back from the stumps, clapped his gloves together and took up his stance. Grace was in his customary position at point where he rocked gently from side to side, becoming aware again of the persistent throbbing in his bruised right heel, and watched Shrewsbury intently as Kortright tore in to bowl the first ball of the match.

Tuesday 19 July 1898

The Champion liked Sir Richard Webster, the Attorney General, a great deal. He had a kind face, with eyes that sparkled in the gas- and candlelight of the Sports Club's dining room in St James's Square. He'd met him many times over the years, most frequently in his capacity as the President of the Surrey county club, and always enjoyed his company. To have Sir Richard preside over his official birthday banquet seemed entirely appropriate.

As Sir Richard prepared to make his remarks and propose the toast, Grace looked at his sore knuckle, opened and closed his fingers and felt the pain shoot across the back of his hand. It hurt more than he'd anticipated after being struck earlier in the day by a ball from Haigh that had leapt from a length and caused him to drop his bat. The hubbub and laughter of the dining room faded into the distance and as he flexed his fingers the events of the day replayed themselves in his mind. It had been a difficult day's batting for the Gentlemen: heavy overnight rain had made the wicket treacherous. He'd opened with Stoddart, a batsman who usually revelled on a sticky wicket, and in poor light they'd found the going very difficult indeed. Jack

Hearne's breaking medium-pacers from the Pavilion End were particularly troublesome.

He was dropped early in the day by Lilley behind the wicket and then saw Hearne just fail to reach a caught and bowled chance soon afterwards. Knowing he could rely on Stoddy at the other end – he recalled the 151 they'd put on in the same fixture three years earlier against the bowling of Richardson and Mold – he'd knuckled down, just playing each ball on its own merits in his usual manner, watching the ball carefully off the pitch, jamming the bat down on shooters, reacting quickly to odd bounces and clever breaks and refusing a runner despite the constant pain in his heel (relying on another man to take his runs for him was, he felt, an added distraction he could do without). The opening pair held out gallantly for an hour before the Middlesex man nicked Lockwood to Alec Hearne with the score on 56. Grace's heel grew more painful but still he ran singles when he could, reaching a hard-fought 43 before cutting Lockwood to Lilley.

In the circumstances he was wholly satisfied with the Gentlemen's 303, pushing the Players' first innings score of 335 close enough to make defeat unlikely. In the final 50 minutes of play Kortright and Woods had removed Shrewsbury and Abel, putting the Gentlemen in a strong position going into the final day, but his painful hand and heel had meant he'd not taken the field.

He was thinking about how much to bowl Kortright in the morning – the Essex man had put in long spells in the first innings at the expense of some of his pace – when he became aware that Sir Richard was leaning over to address him and show him a copy of a telegram. The noise of the room filled his ears again. The guests were boisterous – the occasion was, after all, a merry one – the food had been excellent and the wine waiters were proving as fluent and effective as Jack Hearne had been on today's difficult wicket, albeit less threatening.

'If you are ready, Doctor,' he said, 'I shall commence the toasts presently and say a few words that I hope will be appropriate to this auspicious occasion.'

'I am much obliged, sir, for this honour you have done me,' said the Old Man. 'I'm quite certain that I shall not be worthy of whatever it is you might be about to relate.'

Sir Richard nodded and smiled at him, stood up, tinged his butter knife against his wine glass and waited for the noise to die away amid a breeze of hushes.

'Gentlemen,' he began, 'I trust you have enjoyed the fine fare prepared here this evening in honour of our esteemed guest. I would crave your attention for a few moments and ask you first to stand and raise a toast to … her majesty the Queen.'

Chairs scraped on the floor as some 150 men stood, raised their glasses, echoed the toast and sipped in silence.

'May I also take this opportunity to pay tribute to the Prince and Princess of Wales and the rest of the Royal Family,' he continued. 'You all know what a sterling good sportsman the Prince of Wales is. I have had the privilege of meeting his Royal Highness in sporting circles over the past forty years, and I know that he is as keen about sport today as he ever was. We all deeply regret the serious accident that has befallen him, and express the sincere hope that medical skill will soon restore him to his ordinary condition of health and activity. Gentlemen, I pray you be seated.'

'The Prince has had an accident?' Grace whispered to Stoddart, his neighbour, as the guests retook their seats.

'Slipped and fell on a spiral staircase at Waddesdon Manor, I believe,' came the reply. 'His leg is apparently quite badly broken.'

Stoddart raised an eyebrow and waggled his hand before his lips as if holding an imaginary glass. A smile played briefly on Grace's lips as Sir Richard began to speak again.

'I know of no greater honour than that which has been conferred upon me in being asked to preside on this occasion,' he said, to muted hear-hears. 'When I look round the table and see present such splendid cricketers as Stoddart, Mason and Kortright, Dixon representing the fine old county of Nottinghamshire, Woods, Wynyard, MacGregor, Hill from Somerset, and Murdoch, from Sussex, I feel quite unfit to so much as black their boots. Still, worthy or unworthy, I feel proud to be your spokesman in proposing W.G.'s health.

'I am not going to trouble you with statistics,' he said, to relieved laughter. 'Mr Brown, who instructs me in everything connected with cricket, has provided me with a brief, without, I should say, a fee' – he paused to allow for laughter that never came – 'ah, in which all the doings of W.G. Grace are recounted. I propose, with apologies to Mr Brown, to entirely disregard them. I do have, however, some qualification for speaking to the toast as I already know much of this fine gentleman's career.

'I remember in the sixties talking of E.M. Grace's outstanding performances and being told by a gentleman from Bristol, "Yes, Mr Webster, he is a good cricketer all right. But, mark my words, his younger brother is going to beat him." Since then we have all been aware of the distinction that W.G. Grace has attained in the game. For tonight's occasion a listing of statistics would be inappropriate and would also fail to give you the measure of the man who sits here to my right, a colossus bestriding the wonderful game of cricket.'

A wave of applause washed through the room.

'Let me illustrate his standing with a small anecdote. I am told that a boy was once being examined in a Gloucestershire Sunday school and the master enquired, "What are the Christian graces?" The small boy replied that he knew the three Christian graces surely, and they were E.M., W.G. and G.F.'

The room erupted with laughter and cheers. The Doctor smiled and looked down at the tablecloth.

'Since then the story has had its parallel in another tale told to me recently. An Eton boy was asked what to name the three Christian graces and he replied, "Grace before meat, grace after meat, and W.G. Grace".'

There was more laughter; the Doctor's face creased into a wide, appreciative grin even though he'd heard the story many times before.

'Now, those incidents,' continued Sir Richard, 'though they might be said to be interesting and amusing, are both true and demonstrate the hold which W.G. has had on our hearts for many years. So I am not going to talk about centuries or numbers of wickets, or all those extremely interesting things of which W.G. should be justly proud. Instead I ask you to consider his career from what we might call the *humanising* point of view. There is no man in England who has done more to elevate sport than W.G. This is no idle boast or empty platitude. Indeed, to prove the worth of those words, last night I was sitting on the Treasury Bench and said to Mr Arthur Balfour, First Lord of the Treasury, "I have had a great honour conferred upon me: I am going to preside at W.G.'s dinner tomorrow night", and Balfour said, "Give him my kindest wishes and tell him I am just of the same age as he is, almost to the day." I am certain that 1848 will for ever be celebrated not by the revolution in France, nor by the abdication of Louis-Philippe, but instead it will be remembered for the fact of the birth of W.G. Grace.

'I was not going to speak of W.G. as batsman, bowler, fielder or captain but to tell you instead of the one thing which has struck me with pleasure all through the long years that I have been following cricket with devotion. More than once it has fallen to my lot to know of the kindly words that W.G. Grace has said to young cricketers. Those kindly words, to the schoolboy and the University cricketer, have never been forgotten, and have had a good deal to do with the successful career of those cricketers in the field afterwards. They recognised in Mr Grace large-heartedness, unselfishness and thought for others' – at this Charles Kortright let out a snort – 'and he will be remembered because he has elevated sport, because he played cricket as a sportsman's genie, and has played from beginning to end courageously, honourably and straightforwardly' – here Kortright had a small coughing fit – 'and not simply to make a great many runs, but to make his side play the game as they ought to play it.

'It is not only in cricket that he has made his mark. I well remember a performance of his that remains unique. After making 221 not out at cricket for the Gentlemen of England against Surrey at The Oval in the year 1866, W.G. went to the Crystal Palace and there in the evening won the quarter of a mile over twenty hurdles. That, gentlemen, is the calibre of sportsman we are celebrating here this evening.

'We honour him here tonight because he is a large-hearted Englishman, because he consistently offers the hand of good fellowship to young and old and because he has elevated the national sport of county cricket to its present position.'

He paused as applause and the banging of fists on tables filled the room.

'One day, I suppose,' he continued, 'W.G. will grow old.'

A rumble of denial went around the tables.

'Despite this I hope that in forty or fifty years' time he will be able to reflect on the fact that he has elevated a manly British sport, that he has played cricket honestly as a gentleman and a sportsman without thinking of himself' – at this Kortright nearly bit clean through the stem of his pipe – 'that he has set an example to many a younger man and earned the deserved admiration of the British nation. W.G. Grace is a manly, straightforward English sportsman.'

Sir Richard raised his glass with a flourish and announced, 'Gentlemen, I present to you a man of such renown that he is known best by his initials. W.G.!'

There was a mass scraping of chairs from which emerged a wave of 'W.G.'s in response, followed by a warm and lengthy round of applause.

The Old Man let everyone settle back into their chairs before rising from his seat. Applause and cheering broke out again, this time showing no sign of abating until he was forced to raise his hand in an appeal for silence. Eventually, after what seemed like an age, the tumult died away to nothing and he looked around the room. He hated public speaking. Even after all these years he found it neither easier nor any less of a chore than it had been at the very beginning. Usually he favoured what he termed his 'Canadian speech', a short template he had developed on the MCC tour of the United States and Canada in 1872. 'Gentlemen,' he would begin, 'I beg to thank you for the honour you have done me. I never saw better bowling than I have seen today and I hope to see as good wherever I go.'

'Bowling', he soon realised, could be switched easily with 'batting', 'fielding' or even, if he were feeling extra playful, 'women'. Clearly, the Canadian speech would not have been appropriate on this occasion so he had prepared something a little more substantial, if still agreeably brief.

'Gentlemen,' he said, 'I cannot find the words to express my thanks for your reception tonight and the very kind way in which Sir Richard Webster has just spoken about me. You have truly done me the greatest honour I have ever experienced in my life. When I look around and see the friends and cricketers near me I wish I had my friend Stoddart's happy knack of saying the right words in the right place. If it be that I cannot say the right words, then I certainly feel them.

'As you know, I am a man of few words. When I am pleased those words might be all right, and when I am not they might be all wrong.'

Once the laughter had died away, he continued.

'I hope tonight, therefore, that they are right. Sir Richard Webster has said many kind words about me this evening that I do not deserve. In regard to his reference to the hurdle race at the Crystal Palace I feel I should point out that on the occasion to which he refers five started the race but only one finished, that being myself. That was a lucky one.'

Again laughter washed over him.

'As to cricket, Sir Richard Webster was perhaps not being entirely truthful when he said that I was always kind to young players. I remember an occasion some years ago when in a match at Lord's for MCC against Surrey they brought up an unfortunate youngster who had taken a few wickets at a match the week before. His first ball I played quietly back to him, the second went over into the garden by the old armoury and the third followed suit. The fourth and fifth went into the pavilion and after that they never bowled the poor fellow again. I do not know whether that counts as being kind to young cricketers but I suspect it's not what Sir Richard had in mind.'

Again, laughter and applause filled the room.

'I am very proud to be captain of the lot we have here this evening,' he continued. 'I have played on a good many wickets and know when they are a little bad. I can tell you that to score more than 300 runs on the wicket we have played on against such bowling as we saw today was better than any of us could have expected. Indeed, my old friend Stoddart and I thought we had done pretty well when we got to fifty.

'The 300 wasn't made by one man but by everybody and I must say that if we had won the toss the game would be very nearly over tonight.

'In conclusion, I thank you again for your kind words and deeds on this, the occasion of my fiftieth birthday, and thank you from the very bottom of my heart for the kind way the toast has been both proposed and received.'

He sat down, relieved the ordeal was over, with cheering and applause ringing in his ears that turned into a long standing ovation. He dabbed the sweat from his brow with his napkin, wiped the back of his neck, and when the ovation showed no sign of abating half rose from his chair and inclined his head.

When the applause finally subsided he excused himself from the table and made his way outside for some fresh-air relief from the cigar- and pipe-smoke fug of the dining room. The contrast between the boisterous hullabaloo behind him and the quiet of St James's Square was so great it made his ears ring. He looked across to the darkness of the square, crossed the street, walked to the gravelled octagon in the middle and took a seat on one of the cast-iron benches. He rubbed the back of his sore hand and flexed his fingers for a moment, then bowed his head, looked at the ground and breathed out expansively, enjoying the air and the peace.

Fifty. A half-century. He had never been an introspective man but out here, on his own in the dark with his thoughts, away from the noise and the drunken chatter, he allowed himself a minor nostalgic indulgence. He'd always tried to avoid thinking about his own place in the scheme of things because if he permitted himself to embrace the gushing praise that had been heaped upon him from all sides for decades now it would not make for a healthy mind. He preferred to keep his thoughts simple, avoiding analysis. He worked on his instincts and, importantly, he trusted those instincts. They had, it was inarguable, served him very well.

He'd certainly travelled far from those early days playing with his brothers in the field at Downend, with Uncle Pocock showing him how it was done, and his dear mother, always, in equal measure, her sons' biggest supporter and critic, telling him exactly where he was going wrong.

He thought back to the days when he was younger and slimmer. He surveyed the spread of his stomach. Curiously, he was a careful eater and moderate drinker, and heaven knows he got plenty of exercise, yet once he'd reached the full flush of adulthood his waistline had embarked on a non-stop course of expansion. Fortunately his strength, stamina and agility had prevented this from affecting his cricket, but now he'd reached 50 he was forced to recognise that old age was becoming a factor in his all-round game.

It was mainly in the field that this was obvious. In fact it was only in the field that one could detect any visible evidence of the fast-ticking years beyond the grey flecks in his beard. These days he was far from the demon point fielder he once had been. He would still catch any chance that came to him, no matter how hard it fizzed through the air, but ground work was becoming more and more difficult. He thought back to the caught and bowled he'd taken at Leyton a few days earlier: he'd been so delighted to reach down and take the ball so close to his boots that he not given a thought to whether it was a clean catch or not. His instincts told him it was, and his instincts were what had fuelled all his successes on the cricket field. Either way, the catch was clean enough: the umpire wouldn't have given it if he hadn't been in strong agreement.

In giving credence to the effects of time on his physique he went on to wonder what the future might hold. How much longer could he carry on playing before the years really began to catch up? The thing was, he still *felt* young; still felt the same keen anticipation for a game of cricket that he'd known as a youth, the same tingling excitement in his stomach, the same thrill when he was assailed by the smell of cut grass and linseed oil. Even the musty dampness and stale sweat of the average county dressing-room quickened his pulse as much today as it had back in the sixties.

Enthusiasm was one thing, it was his own level of performance that mattered. Twelve wickets against Somersetshire and that 126 against Essex in the past week confirmed that he was still more than worthy of a place among the very best, but the dull, constant throbbing of his bruised heel and the sharp pains in his injured hand were increasingly persistent reminders, not that he needed them, of his own mortality.

He raised his head, leaned back on the bench and looked up at the sky. It was a clear night with barely a cloud and he could see stars behind the stars as he looked deep into the night's canopy. The universe was opening up before him and suddenly, for a moment, he was just a man with most of his life now behind him, suffering with a sore heel and sitting on a bench feeling very small indeed.

Wednesday 20 July 1898

Kortright walked to the wicket, his bat feeling heavy in his hands. He may have been one of the most feared fast bowlers in the country but as W.G. moved across to intercept him the Old Man could detect anxiety in his eyes. The Gentlemen had collapsed dramatically to 80 for nine with 45 minutes to play. No chance of winning the game but, as far as the Old Man was concerned, every chance of saving it. Jack Hearne's reliable medium-pacers were rearing off a length but as long as the batsman got himself in line and played correctly there shouldn't be much danger, even for a tailender like Kortright.

The Players had been dismissed in their second innings for 263 on a wicket that was behaving much better than it had the previous day, Billy Gunn adding 56 to his magnificent first innings of 139 and Bill Storer top scoring with 73. W.G. had sat out the Players' innings with his bruised heel and swollen hand and, with two and a half hours to play, a victory for the Gentlemen was all but out of the question and the match looked likely to end in a draw. However, Jack Hearne had torn through the Gentlemen's early order leaving them 56 for six, the Middlesex man making the ball break on the drying wicket by anything up to nine inches. Having planned to sit out the innings on the grounds of his bruised heel and hand and the fact that the game could be saved without his assistance, the Champion had waited until the seventh wicket fell at 77 with an hour still to play before finally walking to the wicket. Dixon, at the other end, was bowled almost immediately and MacGregor followed three runs later (meaning that apart from Stoddart's, the first to fall, every wicket in the innings had been clean bowled).

The previous animosity with Kortright didn't even enter Grace's mind as he approached the wicket: there was a game to be saved along with the honour of the Gentlemen and that was all that mattered. They had exchanged a few cursory phrases while in the field where a level of contact between captain and strike bowler was essential, but now, in fading light, with three-quarters of an hour still to play, the two antagonists found themselves batting together to save the match. Grace was ready for the struggle: after all, this was his jubilee match and he had no intention of being on the losing side. In his mind it was down to how Kortright coped with the situation.

The pair met at the edge of the square.

'Don't be nervous now, Korty,' he said, 'just play your natural game.'

'All right, Doc,' replied the Essex man, 'I'll do my best.'

Kortright took guard, looked around the field and was ready. Hearne came in off his short, skippy run and with his smooth, classical action sent down a ball on a good length. Kortright played down the wrong line and the ball came within a whisker of clipping his off stump. The cry of the close fielders was followed to the middle a second later by the mass exhalation of the capacity Lord's crowd. But he'd survived.

His advice to Kortright may have sounded trite, patronising even, but it was sincere. In the Doctor's mind there were few situations that called for anything else but playing one's natural game. It's what had served him best throughout his career and was entirely responsible for him being here, two days into his 51st year, at the wicket in front of a packed Lord's crowd there for a match played in his honour. To him cricket, and batting in particular, was a simple game and he couldn't fathom why people would wish to complicate it: all one had to do was treat each delivery as an individual entity and deal with it accordingly. The moment the ball left the bowler's hand nothing else mattered beyond what happened when it arrived 20 yards down the wicket. In that instant the score was irrelevant, the identity of the bowler was irrelevant, the location was irrelevant. Once that ball was in flight all one had to do was watch it, establish where it would pitch and play a shot accordingly. That was all that mattered. The moment.

Lockwood came charging in and sent down a fizzing delivery outside off stump. W.G. got himself in line, head over the ball and blocked it towards mid-off. The next delivery was identical, with the same outcome. The third was pitched up on the line of off stump. With scant movement of the feet, indeed, little movement of anything but those great meaty arms, the Doctor swung straight and through the ball. As soon as he made contact, however, the vibrations shimmering through his forearms told him the ball had not risen as much as he'd anticipated and hit a much lower part of the bat than he would have liked. He looked up to see it arcing through the azure blue of the sky and as he began lumbering through for the single, the soreness in his heel slowing him more than usual, he lowered his gaze to see Bobby Abel, his cap flying off as he ran towards the ball, arms out in front of him, in pursuit of the catch that would win the game.

The Doctor concentrated on making good his ground rather than Abel closing in on the dropping ball. His eyes were fixed firmly on the crease as he lumbered towards completing the run and, as he'd suspected would happen, the gasp of the crowd told him the little Surrey man hadn't quite made up the ground. He heard Abel's apology, then the smack of the ball into Lockwood's hands at the end of his run and someone call out, 'Hard luck, Bobby!'

The tension was palpable among the fielders and the crowd and only increased as the minutes ticked slowly by. Grace was immune to it, of course, and if Kortright was feeling the pressure the Old Man was pleased to note that he certainly wasn't showing it, playing straight and clipping the occasional wide delivery through the covers to the boundary with increasing confidence. The pain in Grace's heel meant he turned down more singles than he took and was soon outscored by his partner but, soreness aside, he still hobbled through for the odd run after hits into the deep as well as sending the occasional loose delivery fizzing to the boundary. Regardless of the situation, if a ball deserved to be hit then he would always hit it.

Eventually Arthur Shrewsbury grew desperate enough to throw the ball to Bill Storer, an occasional bowler charitably described as a leg-spinner. The clock was running down and the batsmen were well set: Grace had noted with satisfaction the jitteriness creeping into the fielding and how the chatter among them when he'd walked out to bat had long since ceased. The fielders were tenser than the batsmen and that was the way he liked it.

As the clock ticked over to 6.30 the Old Man looked on approvingly as Kortright resisted an entire over of inviting long-hops from Storer, patting each of them gently back to the bowler, before putting his bat under his arm and beginning to trot lightly back towards the Pavilion.

Grace's eyes twinkled.

'Not so fast, Korty, there's half an hour yet,' he said as the beaming Essex man approached him.

'Six thirty finish, Doctor, surely?' came the incredulous reply as Kortright's smile fell from his face so quickly Grace almost heard it hit the ground.

'Arthur and I agreed we'd play until seven if there was still a chance of a result,' he said. 'Back you go, just keep playing as you were and we shall have no trouble.'

Kortright's shoulders drooped slightly as he walked back to the crease. The Old Man had done it to him again, but at least this time he could see method in it. If he'd gone out knowing there was an hour and a quarter to play rather than 45 minutes he may not have lasted as long as he had. Another half-hour, then. So be it.

To his credit Kortright kept his head down and batted on sensibly, accumulating runs from bad balls and blocking the good ones, with Grace doing likewise at the other end. So bonded had the two men become in their fierce resilience that with 20 minutes to play Grace walked up the wicket between overs and held out his hand. Without hesitation Kortright shook it. No words were spoken, their eyes barely met, but their antagonism had been entirely extinguished by their increasingly extraordinary batting partnership.

It was four minutes before seven o'clock when Lockwood returned at the Pavilion End. Kortright took strike, the low sun in his eyes. They'd batted together for nearly an hour and a half now, almost exactly doubling the total, and Kortright had scored 46, easily the highest score of the innings. The first two deliveries were straight, quick, well-pitched up and blocked by Kortright with solid defensive strokes, the second presenting such a formidable defence that W.G. let out a spontaneous, 'Oh, well played, well played' from the non-striker's end. The third ball was slower, pitching on a length outside off stump. Confident now, the job all but done, and perhaps sensing a rare opportunity for a half-century, Kortright swished at the ball, catching it low on the bat and watching in horror as it curled through the air to disappear into the huge, safe Yorkshire hands of Schofield Haigh running around from cover. Kortright looked at the sky and roared his frustration. The crowd, spellbound and silent until now, broke into loud applause in appreciation of the result but also of the remarkable effort of the last pair at the wicket.

As he walked slowly from the wicket, dragging his bat behind him, Kortright still couldn't meet Grace's eye.

'I'm sorry, Doc,' he said, 'I thought it was one to hit.'

'Well played, Korty,' came the reply. 'You played your natural game, I asked for nothing more.'

With that he took Kortright's arm and the two of them set off for the Pavilion, disappearing into a cheering throng of three-piece suits, watch chains and straw boaters. They eventually reached the gate, went up the steps together through a forest of silk hats and disappeared into the Long Room. Making their way to the dressing-room, still arm in arm, they found the rest of the team waiting for them, standing and applauding to a man. The doors on to the balcony were open and the applause and cheering from below washed up over the balcony in waves.

'Come on, Korty,' said Grace, 'out we go.' He knew the Essex man would be blaming himself for losing the match but, if he was honest with himself, he'd have played exactly the same shot. He'd have timed it better, of course, but he wasn't going to blame the man for it, Korty wasn't a batsman and had already played out of his skin, and Grace was determined nobody else would blame him either.

He ushered the Essex man on to the balcony where the crowd gave them a huge reception. Finally, Kortright broke into a smile and waved. The Doctor did likewise. In different ways he and Kortright had finished the game either side of fifty.

Saturday 12 November 1898

There was a knock at the study door. 'Come in,' he said, and the door opened.

'Ah, hello, Porritt, have a seat.'

Only the most eagle-eyed would have noticed the slight stoop to Arthur Porritt's shoulders on entering the room. When the publisher James Bowden had asked him if he'd care to undertake the writing of W.G.'s memoirs he'd been as delighted as he was excited. This was a terrific opportunity. Everyone knew W.G. Grace; there was barely a person in the land, let alone a cricket enthusiast, who couldn't identify him by his immense height, girth and beard. So great was his reputation and so well-known his unique appearance that he was almost, in the public sense, a caricature of himself. That was what motivated Porritt: that people only knew the caricature. If everybody knew W.G., how many could say they really, truly *knew* W.G.? Here was the best opportunity yet to look behind the curtain of the public face and share the real man with the reading public, his motivations, his methods, his beliefs, his hopes and dreams and desires, so that they might know what lay behind the familiar façade of cricketing genius. Yes, Porritt thought, he was the man for the job. As an interviewer of some experience he was just the fellow to extract the great man's innermost thoughts. Far from being a trite memoir of platitudes and statistics, this book would be a landmark of biography. While the name W.G. Grace on the spine would guarantee sales, Porritt had set out to make this a book of genuine substance, a book whose content would ensure its longevity rather than a brief burst of publicity and sales before a plummet towards the back shelves of the antiquarian book dealers. This, this, would be a keeper.

Except it wasn't really working out that way. While he had been delighted to find that Grace had terrific recall and a comprehensive collection of records and statistics at his fingertips in books, annuals and journals, it was when Porritt tried to coax him beyond the bare facts of his achievements, to get beneath the skin of the Champion, that the problems began. There was nothing. He was a blank canvas presented as a finished work. Whenever he tried to push his subject for more detail, more nuance, more W.G., he'd be greeted with nothing more than a few rapid blinks and the reassertion of the basic facts just established in a manner that suggested Grace believed the writer had temporarily lost his hearing.

Perhaps today would be different, he'd thought. Today he wanted to talk about Grace's 100th hundred, made three years earlier against Somerset at Bristol in Grace's 47th year. Surely such a milestone would elicit more than a cursory summary and give the book some depth. W.G. watched as Porritt opened his briefcase and took out his notebook. He rested his hands on his stomach and swung gently back and forth on his chair. He liked Porritt. It was a good job he did, too, as this book business was becoming a frightful chore. He wasn't sure why anyone might want to read a reworking of his playing career when such information was available elsewhere – and he'd covered quite a lot of the same ground in *Cricket* seven years earlier – but the money he'd negotiated from the publisher was more than enough to warrant passing a few afternoons in Porritt's agreeable company. The man did ask an infernal amount of silly questions, though.

'How are you this afternoon, Doctor?' asked Porritt.

'Oh, not too bad thank you, Porritt,' he answered. 'We're settling into the house now and living in London isn't all that different to what I'm used to.'

'London County has you well provided for here, Doctor, it's a beautiful house.'

'It will suffice for now, yes. Sydenham is convenient for my son Charles, too, as he is to study engineering close to the Crystal Palace. Now, shall we begin?'

Much as he enjoyed Porritt's company he did not wish to prolong the encounter with small talk.

'Annie will bring us some tea presently.'

Porritt crossed his legs and smoothed his notebook against his thigh.

'That's most kind, thank you. I thought this afternoon we might talk about your hundredth century, Doctor, if that suits?'

'A memorable day, Porritt, a memorable day indeed,' he said, leaning forward in his chair. 'Now: it was a match against Somerset, at Ashley Down, would have been three years ago in May. They batted first; I think we lost the toss but we bowled them out for around 300, I took five wickets, one of their openers got a hundred. Fowler, I think it was, but I'm sure you can check that. We had to bat for about an hour, I think, at the end of the day and lost two early wickets but my godson Townsend and I saw us through to the close.

'Come the next day we put on more than 200, if I recall correctly, and I think I do, before Charles was out just short of his century. I went on to get 288 and we won the match by nine wickets.'

He sat back in his chair, pleased with himself. It was an important landmark and one people would be interested in: Porritt would be able to put a little flesh on the bones, but he was pleased with what he remembered of it off the top of his head.

Porritt was looking at him, expectantly, as if he would continue. There was a tap at the door and Annie brought in the tea tray, placing it on the table between them.

'Thank you, Annie,' said the Doctor.

'Yes, thank you,' echoed Porritt, before looking back at him with the same expression of expectation.

'Annie came up to London with us from Bristol,' said Grace. 'She's practically one of the family, aren't you, Annie?'

'Thank you, Doctor,' she replied shyly as she left the room, 'it was most kind of you to keep me in your employ.'

'We also inherited my wife's elderly Aunt Caroline,' said Grace in a low voice, raising his eyes to the ceiling to indicate her presence upstairs, 'but you can't have everything, I suppose. Don't write that down, Porritt.'

The journalist smiled.

'I'm sure she's as fine a lady as your wife, Doctor,' he said. 'But back to the subject of our discussion, if I may. Your hundredth century. How did it feel to reach that astonishing milestone?'

'Well, if I recall correctly, I brought up my century by hitting a full toss from Sammy Woods to the mid-off boundary.'

'And what went through your mind as the ball went to the boundary?'

'I knew it was hit well enough that I wouldn't need to run.'

Frustration flickered fleetingly across Porritt's brow like the shadow of a bird flying past a window. Grace didn't notice.

'You must have been elated? Or perhaps relieved?'

'I was happy, of course I was. I was also pleased that my godson was batting at the other end and was thus the first to shake my hand. With the match being at Bristol my brothers were also there, as well as my Uncle Pocock. When I reached my double-century, E.M. sent a magnum of champagne out to the wicket.'

'But ... surely there must be more you can tell me, about how it actually *felt*?'

He was a little surprised at Porritt's persistence. Had he not already told him he was happy?

'It was my highest score since 1876, Porritt, when I made 318 against Yorkshire, so as well as my hundredth century it was a memorable innings in its own right.'

'But what was going through your *mind*, Doctor? Were you nervous approaching the hundred?'

Faint hackles of irritation began to rise in Grace at Porritt's inexplicable persistence.

'I can't rightly recall,' he said a little sharply. 'You must understand that I am fifty years old, Porritt, I have played many innings in my time and scored a great number of runs from a great number of deliveries on a great number of pitches. I can't be expected to give a ball-by-ball account of each of them because I don't remember them all. They just sort of blend into one.'

'Of course, Doctor, I don't expect you to recall every ball or even every over, but with it being such an important and auspicious landmark for you, and indeed the game of cricket in general, I think your readers would very much enjoy any insight you can give them into what the experience actually felt like. People want to put themselves in the place of W.G. Grace as he was making that hundredth century, what thoughts were in his mind, what the whole experience of such a big innings and extraordinary landmark means to W.G. Grace as a man and as a batsman.'

Grace was silent for a few moments.

'I want to help you, Porritt, truly I do,' he said, 'but to be perfectly honest with you I did not feel anything. I had too much to do watching the bowling and seeing how the fieldsmen were moved about to think anything. It's as simple as that.

'I'd reached the late nineties and was finding it difficult to get the ball away due to some fine bowling. Then dear old Sammy Woods served me up a full toss and I drove it to the boundary just as I would any other full toss in any other game in any other situation. I don't know what else I can tell you. I was happy, as I'm always happy to make a big score. The crowd gave me a great cheer, everyone on the field shook my hand and then I marked my guard again and prepared for the next delivery. I got my head down, my eye was in and I went on to make 288, my highest score in a long time. It was all very satisfactory and crucial to our going on to win the game convincingly. Now, will you have some tea and we shall talk of the next subject?'

Tuesday 6 February 1899

He opened the door from the drawing room into the garden, stepped down on to the gravel and fell to his knees. All was still but for the tendrils of cold now working their way between the buttons of his shirt; icy fingers that felt their way over his collar and down the back of his neck, that wound between his bare toes and between his fingers. Breath clouds formed in front of his face, drifting up and away into the pre-dawn. The Old Man looked up at the deep royal blue above the skeletal trees, spread his arms wide, opened his mouth and let out a guttural roar of uncontained anguish.

He toppled forward on to his hands and tears fell on to the stones. Not Bessie, not his Bessie, please, not his Bessie. Of all the children, she had gladdened his heart the most, lifting his spirits every time she entered a room, giggling as he grabbed her and pulled her to him, planting a kiss on her blood-flushed cheek. The sun shone in his heart when Bessie was around; her smile, her laugh, the way she embraced life and then wrung it out for all its goodness and worth.

The sight of her so pale in that bed, the pink rash across her stomach when she kicked off the blankets and wrenched at her nightdress, the muttering, the sweat,

the fever and the gradual fading away until that moment
a few minutes ago when the muttering, the twitching
and the breathing stopped and she was still. All was still.
The stillness spread steadily through the entire house
and he had to get out, to escape the stifling nothingness.
Even here, outside, the air was still and nothing moved,
as if the life leaving Bessie had caused everything to stop,
as if the world no longer turned, as if the last vestiges of
the night's darkness would never lift. The realisation that
this day would soon begin in earnest and begin without
Bessie tore at his heart. She had left the world in darkness
when in life she'd carried her light everywhere she went.

Bessie was the child who reminded him most of
himself. Her infectious laughter as she'd bowled
underarm to him in the garden at Downend as a child,
the heart-bursting pride he'd felt watching her score a
half-century at 15 years old for the Ladies of Clifton
against the Ladies of Glamorgan, playing exuberant
shots all around the wicket in a way that others noted
was reminiscent of himself. He thought of the tears in
her eyes when he'd first seen her after making his 100th
century. She'd even smiled and stroked his face when
he'd told her on her 17th birthday the time had come
for her to stop playing cricket as it was a game for girls
that was too vulgar for grown women, and she never
even mentioned the subject again.

He remembered the coldness in his stomach that day
just before Christmas when first he'd realised what was

causing her fever. He'd brought in a colleague for another opinion, hoping against hope that he was mistaken, but within seconds of seeing her the man had taken off his spectacles, looked away from W.G.'s imploring eyes, given one shake of his head, touched him lightly on the forearm and left without a word.

He'd sat with her most afternoons, watching the light of youth fade gradually from her grey-green eyes, watching her become someone and something he didn't recognise as his brilliant, life-giving Bessie. He'd tried to smile as she'd looked at him with empty eyes, tried to keep her spirits up with talk of recovery and the forthcoming season, but he knew, and worst of all he knew that *she* knew. He'd seen typhoid knock the fight out of people in his years of practice among the poor of Bristol; when the fight went out of Bessie, the supreme fighter of them all, when her body became so limp and her murmurs so fatigued, he knew the end was close. He'd hoped and prayed for a turnaround, that the sheer force of her personality would surge through to conquer the infection, but deep down he knew all hope was gone.

'For the Lord's sake come inside, Gilbert, this is no time to be out there.'

Agnes's voice quivered and cracked behind him. He heaved his bulk upright and turned to see her in the doorway, one hand on the frame, even in the morning gloaming her eyes visibly red-rimmed and dark. She turned and went back inside, to the gloom and stillness of the house.

He stood for a moment, glanced up at the dark window of Bessie's room, wiped irritably at his cheek with the back of his hand and then followed, pushing the door closed behind him.

Sunday 28 May 1899

He was still seething. For two days he'd read and reread the letter and still he couldn't believe the nerve of them. He'd left it on the top of a pile of correspondence on the desk in his study but all weekend had kept returning to it, as if hoping it might say something different after all.

'How dare they? How *dare* they?' he railed at Agnes, who knew just the appropriate noises to make in reply. Even when he wasn't actually saying anything he was brooding, muttering, pursing his lips and tugging at his beard. She'd seen him in funks over the years, usually regarding some umpiring decision, but this time she could practically see lightning playing about his temples. They were both still grieving for Bessie. Her death was still raw and the house still felt as though there were a vacuum where Bessie should be. Agnes knew that her husband's anger was fuelled at least in part by the broken heart he still nursed for his daughter and made allowances accordingly.

She'd been glad that he'd had the organisation of the new London County club to occupy his time before the season commenced; it gave him a focus. It was, of course, the reason why they'd moved from Bristol altogether once his general practice had ended with the redrawing of the parish union boundaries and he and other GPs had resigned in protest. But since they had arrived he'd thrown himself into the London County job, becoming involved in every aspect of the new club from supervising the construction of the pavilion to engaging the old Gloucestershire bowler Murch as a ground professional. He'd even seen to the lopping of tree branches that threw shadows across the wicket once the sun began to sink.

London County had won their first match convincingly three weeks earlier, beating Wiltshire by six wickets at Swindon, then earned a very creditable draw with the touring Australians at the Palace. They'd had to call themselves the South of England rather than London County in order for the match to be considered first class, but all the same the crowds turned out in great numbers and *The Times* compared the playing surface favourably with that of Lord's and The Oval.

He'd always been a man of drive and energy, thought Agnes; it was one of the things that had attracted her to him in the first place despite the awkward gait and curiously high-pitched voice, but it was almost as if he were pushing himself extra hard now for the sake of Bessie. Perhaps he was even punishing himself somehow, for not being able to save her despite his own medical training and expertise.

Agnes had been one of the most enthusiastic advocates of his acceptance of the London County post; she'd urged him to accept it, which served to make his current diligence part of the grieving process. For Gloucestershire to cast a shadow over all that with their extraordinary communication, well, it was absolutely outrageous and she could quite understand his searing resentment.

Grace himself struggled to process the slight in his mind. He'd never known anything like it before. The Gloucestershire committee had sent him a letter demanding to know how many matches he was intending to play for them in the coming season. Him! The captain! The man who, more than any other, had put the county on the cricket map! They presumed to ask *him* about his commitment to the team and the club? Who on earth did they presume to think they were? Granted, he lived in the London suburbs now and had what was effectively a full-time job administering and captaining the London County club, but he'd given them absolutely no grounds to believe this would affect in any way his commitment to Gloucestershire. Why, they'd never pursed their lips at any of his other commitments, such as when he played for the Gentlemen, the Gentlemen of the South or even his own W.G. Grace's XI, so why should the beggars start complaining now? It was an outrage to call into question his commitment, an absolute outrage. Further, it was undignified and the most dreadful impertinence. What made it worse was that he realised the decision had been taken at a committee meeting on 16 May and he'd played two matches for Gloucestershire since then. Two! And nobody had given him any hint or suggestion as to what would be waiting for him in his postbag that Friday morning.

One thing was certain: if they'd really seen fit to issue him with an ultimatum then, by heaven, they would have his answer to it.

It wasn't until Sunday evening that he felt composed enough to draft a response, but even then his pen pressed so hard it repeatedly tore through the paper. A scattering of screwed-up sheets accumulated on the floor around his desk until finally, with a scrawl of his signature, he sat back and read over his response.

'To the Committee of the Gloucestershire County Club,' it began.

Gentlemen. In answer to yours of the 26th, re resolution passed on the 16th and kept back from me for reasons best known to yourselves, I beg to state that I had intended to play in nearly all our matches, but in consequence of the resolution passed and some other actions of some of the Committee, I send in my resignation as captain, and must ask the Committee to choose the teams for future games as I shall not get them up.

I have always tried my very best to promote the interests of the Gloucestershire County Club, and it is with deep regret that I resign the captaincy. I have the greatest affection for the county of my birth, but for the Committee as a body, the greatest contempt.

I am, yours truly,
W.G. Grace

He reread the letter three times before bundling it into the envelope. The final sentence was very strong and they wouldn't like it one bit. But then they weren't meant to like it. In addition it was, of course, entirely true. The committee had proved itself to be a gathering of jumped-up blackguards and charlatans well deserving of his contempt. He'd helped to found the club in the first place and had been its talisman and bedrock for more than 30 years. How could anyone question his commitment and service to the club with which he was most associated? He sealed the envelope, addressed it, held it in both hands for a moment, tapped it a couple of times, placed it on top of the pile of letters to be sent the following morning, walked out of the study and endeavoured to dissipate the remnants of his anger at the billiard table.

Saturday 3 June 1899

The train rattled through the East Midlands, and Grace sat with his back to the engine. Yorkshire's Stanley Jackson sat opposite, smoking his pipe and reading the evening newspaper. The sun was setting out of the left-hand window and the Old Man watched as it lowered itself gently towards the fields, lending a pinkish fringe to the strands of cirrus high in the sky. The light streaming into the carriage grew more golden with each passing minute.

He thought about the Test match just passed. An honourable draw that had looked, at 19 for four, as if it was heading towards a calamitous defeat. Thank heaven for Ranji and his exquisitely crafted 93 not out from a total of 155 for seven at the close.

For once it was his own performance that concerned him. His captaincy had been sound, he thought. He'd bowled young Rhodes extensively, and the youngster on his debut had seven wickets from the match to show for it. Jack Hearne had been as reliable as ever, nearly 90 overs he'd bowled. Grace hadn't put on one of his better showings with the bat. His 28 in the first innings gave England a good grounding of 75 with Charlie Fry for the first wicket, on which the rest of the team, with the exception of Ranji with 42, had failed to capitalise.

In the second innings, however, with the match there to be saved, he'd contributed only a single before a sharp ball from Howell pierced his defence and knocked back his off stump.

It was in the field that, for the first time, he truly felt the years catching up with him. He was, after all, approaching his 51st birthday: few men of his age were even playing outdoor sports beyond a round of golf and the hounds. However, the agile cover point of his youth had now been reduced to standing in position and stopping only those balls that came as near as dammit straight at him. In the Australians' first innings he'd been only too aware of the catcalls of the crowd whenever the ball had sped past him and he'd failed to chase it. The very principle of an English crowd jeering the English captain angered him. They'd been quick enough to cheer the sharp reaction catch he'd taken in the second innings to dismiss Clem Hill, but he if he was honest with himself he was becoming something of a passenger in the field. The ground, he'd told Jackson at the start of the journey, was getting further away these days.

He was still more than worth his place as captain, batsman and bowler – he'd made a handsome 175 for London County against Worcestershire just before the Test – but in the field he wasn't making the contribution he should and with Test cricket improving notably in standard year on year there was little room for surplus players in the field. Although he was justifiably angry at the crowd's reaction to his fielding, he couldn't deny it had stung him. It was a damned impertinence, and he would never allow the derision of spectators to influence any decision he might make, but as the train barrelled through the flat lands of the east of England he debated with himself whether he was letting down his team-mates. The fielders either side of him were having to do his running as well as their own duties and, important figure to the team as he was, that wasn't necessarily fair to them.

This was to be a five-Test summer, too, the first time a series would be contested over so many matches. He would be 51 years old in a little over a month and, while his eye and his arm were as sharp and effective as they had ever been, his legs were not lasting the pace as they should. In that opening partnership with Fry he knew that many of the singles they ran could have been twos had his partner not been conscious of the Doctor's glacial pace between the wickets.

No, the team had to come first. If he wasn't making the kind of contribution in every aspect of the game worthy of a Test match player, let alone the captain, then he had no right to be there. He could make the runs, take the wickets, captain the side and take catches if the ball flew within reach, but if he couldn't chase down the ball in the field nor take what could be crucial singles in a close game then his place should legitimately be in doubt.

The sky had developed a purplish hue and the sun was now a deep orange as its lower circumference flattened against the horizon. Grace turned to look across at Jackson, face hidden behind his newspaper, pipe smoke rising gently above the top of the page.

'It's all over, Jacker,' he said. 'I shan't play again.'

Sunday 11 June 1899

A week and a day later, having made a steady half-century for MCC against the Australians at Lord's in the meantime, he walked through the door of the Sports Club in St James's Square for the meeting of the selectors to pick the team for the second Test, also to be played at Lord's. When he entered the room only Lord Hawke and H.W. Bainbridge, the Warwickshire captain, were present. No matter.

'Gentlemen,' he said before they had taken their seats, 'first things first so we can then get on with the serious business of picking the team. I have decided that I shall retire from the England team and stand down from the captaincy with immediate effect. I feel that while I could hold down a place on the strength of my batting and bowling, in the field the ground has become too damned far away for me to warrant my future participation in Test matches and the time has come to make way for others.'

Hawke and Bainbridge looked at each other in shock, then turned back to look at Grace.

'Gilbert, my dear fellow,' said Hawke, 'you can't be serious?'

'I am quite serious, Hawke, and believe me I have given this matter a great deal of thought.'

'But, Doctor, you are the mainstay of the side, its very bedrock,' squeaked Bainbridge.

'I was, Bainbridge, and in some ways I still am, but I must think of the overall benefit to the team of my continued presence and I do not contribute enough in the field. Gentlemen, do not attempt to dissuade me; you know me well enough to be apprised that my mind is not for changing.'

'Doctor, please reconsider,' said Hawke. 'For your batting alone your place is assured.'

'Please, Hawke, do me the honour of accepting my decision and we can then progress to selecting the team for the forthcoming Test.'

And so the conversation continued, with both Hawke and Bainbridge intent on forcing a change of heart upon the greatest cricketer in the land and Grace as determined in defence as he'd ever been, playing each salvo back to the respective bowler with a sturdily dead bat until C.B. Fry walked into the room gushing apologies for his lateness.

'Here's Charles,' said Grace, with renewed vigour. 'Now, Charles, before you sit down, we want you to answer this question with a yes or a no.'

Lord Hawke made as if to speak, but Grace silenced him with a raised hand.

'Do you think that Archie MacLaren should play in the next Test match?'

'Yes,' replied Fry as he sat down at the table, 'yes, I do.'

'That settles it, then,' said Grace, drawing his hands together on the table top. 'There is not room in the team for both MacLaren and myself. Now, to the next matter, who shall captain the side?'

At the end of the evening Grace was the last to leave, deliberately so. He crossed the road and found the same bench on which he had sat a year earlier. It was a warm night, and a clear one. The Champion looked ahead of him into the darkness and ruminated briefly upon his decision. It was the correct one, unquestionably, for there was no room for sentiment when it came to choosing the England XI. The reluctance, nay, the horror, with which his fellow selectors had greeted his decision gave him a small amount of satisfaction, but they were never going to persuade him into changing his mind.

There would be no farewell appearance, no hullabaloo like that which had greeted his 50th birthday, but that was no matter. It was a shame that his last Test innings for England would forever remain that ignominious single at Trent Bridge, but his record overall would speak for itself.

He leaned his head back, stroked his beard and looked at the stars. They were particularly bright tonight, he thought. And they were quite beautiful. He stayed that way for a few moments, head raised blinking at the heavens. One of them, he noted, seemed slightly brighter than the others and looked to be almost pulsing, as if trying to catch his attention. He smiled to himself, said, 'Goodnight, Bessie', stood up and went in search of a cab.

Saturday 22 August 1903

Dinner the previous evening had been an agreeably upbeat affair. Bertie Lawton acted as host even though they were staying at his father's Cromford house just outside Matlock Bath, and he was understandably in fine form: he'd just played a crucial role in Derbyshire beating Grace's London County side by eight wickets despite having lost the first day's play to rain. Although the margin of victory was great, the finish had been a close-run and thrilling thing: once London County had been bowled out for the second time Derbyshire only had an hour to score the 69 needed to win. Lawton scored more than half the runs which, added to his 55 in the first innings and the seven wickets he'd taken in the match, ensured he was in buoyant mood.

His distinguished guest was a little more reserved. The Doctor had not shown the sparse crowd his best form with the bat: he'd been fortunate on two occasions in the first innings not to be caught when the ball fell just short of the fielders and was even luckier when caught in the slips off a no-ball. Eventually Lawton spreadeagled his stumps for 20, while in the second innings he was out leg before to his host for 21 having just driven him to the long-off boundary the previous ball. It had been, he rued, about the only shot he'd timed right in the whole match.

'How that umpire gave me out leg before I'll never know, Bertie,' he said over the cheese board, 'for that ball was missing my leg stump by about a foot.'

'Ah, come now, Doctor, I wouldn't have appealed if I hadn't been certain and that ball was going on to hit middle and leg stumps,' replied Lawton, before adding, mischievously, 'indeed, the ball was heading almost precisely for the spot on the stumps where I bowled you out in the first innings.'

Grace suppressed a slight rising of hackles and relaxed, offering a thin smile. He liked Lawton a great deal and saw a bright future for the lad. In addition, he was his weekend guest and it would be ill-mannered of him to lose his temper with the man at his dinner table.

'Bertie,' he said, 'I am not disputing your conviction that you had me. But your conviction is quite misplaced on this occasion as the ball was comfortably missing leg. Had justice been served it is likely we would be toasting an honourable draw tonight rather than a Derbyshire victory.'

Lawton chuckled. He knew well Grace's antipathy for being given out leg before and knew he had never once walked off the field after being dismissed in that fashion satisfied he was out, and rather enjoyed a little affectionate teasing of the Champion.

'Ah, Doctor, it is most gratifying to see that your will to win – or at least, not to lose – is as strong as it ever was. May it remain ever so.'

He raised his glass.

'I speak only the truth, Bertie. These old eyes have seen enough cricket balls coming down a cricket pitch to know whether they're going to hit the stumps or not.'

'It's a pity then, Doctor, that your pad obstructed the path of that delivery because then we'd have known for sure that it was going to hit the stumps.'

Grace could see that the discussion, light-hearted as it was, was destined to go round in circles. He was keen to adjourn to the billiard table and so smiled and raised his glass to Lawton in a manner that he considered did not concede the argument in the slightest.

'What do you think, Jessie?' asked Lawton. Grace turned his head and looked to the far end of the table at Lawton's sister Jessie, dark-haired and pretty with eyes that sparkled in the light of the candelabras.

'I'm sure I'm wholly unqualified to comment, Bertie,' she said with a smile, 'especially when it comes to questioning the judgment of Dr Grace.'

Lawton addressed Grace again.

'Jessie is a very fine bowler, Doctor. She captains the Derwent Ladies and has taken many wickets for them this season.'

Grace inclined his head at Jessie. He didn't really approve of grown women playing cricket; he found it undignified, vulgar even. Yet at the same time he recognised something of Bessie in this girl: the liveliness, the way she brimmed with youthful vigour, her outgoing personality, her happy countenance. He felt a sudden yawning in his soul, the emptiness at his very core that manifested itself whenever he thought of Bessie.

'Were you at Derby today, Miss Lawton?' he asked.

'I was, sir, yes,' she replied, 'although my viewing position was at midwicket when your wicket fell so I am afraid I shall have to decline offering an opinion on the veracity of the umpire's decision.'

'I'm very disappointed to hear it,' he replied. 'And what is it that you bowl for the Derwent Ladies?'

'Oh, nothing special, sir,' she answered, 'I'm just delighted if I can pitch the ball somewhere near the wicket.'

'Jessie is being far too modest, Doctor,' interjected Lawton. 'She is able to make the ball break as much as many bowlers whom we have both encountered in the first-class game. She has castled me on numerous occasions over the years since we were children. I fear I may have taught her too well for my own good.'

'If she's even half as fine a bowler as you, Bertie, then she will be a formidable prospect for any batsman.'

'I would love to see Jessie bowling to you, Doctor.'

This was a new voice in the conversation. Clement Edwards, the trade unionist, journalist and cricket enthusiast, was also spending the weekend at Cromford.

Grace wasn't a great admirer of the politically minded of any persuasion but Edwards had seemed an agreeable enough fellow so far.

'I would be most interested in seeing her bowl myself, Mr Edwards,' he replied, 'but I fear the opportunity will never arise.'

'We could make the opportunity arise,' said Lawton. 'In the morning we could pitch stumps on Cromford Meadows and Jessie could pit her wits against you, Doctor.'

'I'm sure Miss Lawton has far better things to do than give up her Sunday morning to bowl at an old man.'

'On the contrary, Dr Grace,' said Jessie, her voice brimming with enthusiasm, 'it would be a great honour to bowl to you.'

'Would a wager convince you, Doctor?' asked Edwards. 'I have seen Miss Lawton bowl and she is as good as Bertie says. I'd be happy to wager a sovereign that in twelve deliveries the lady would strike your wicket once.'

Grace bridled inwardly at this. Clean bowled by a woman? Why, some of the finest bowlers in the game had never penetrated his defences, why would a woman be deemed a good enough bowler to dismiss him? The very insult behind the suggestion prompted him to accept the wager.

'A sovereign you say, Mr Edwards? Very well, I shall be honoured to face the bowling of Miss Lawton tomorrow but I fear you have lost your sovereign.'

Lawton clapped his hands together, rubbed them and rose from his chair.

'That's settled then,' he said. 'Let us convene at noon at Cromford Meadows and we shall see whether Jessie has the guile and craft to bowl out the great W.G. Grace inside twelve deliveries. Now, gentlemen, shall we adjourn for some billiards? My father has a rather good brandy in the games room that I am anxious for you to try.'

The next day was hot and sunny as Grace took guard at the wicket. He looked down the pitch to where Bertie Lawton acted as umpire and Jessie stood slightly to one side ready to bowl. Clement Edwards and a gaggle of other guests had gathered behind the Champion and a trickle of curious locals spread around the boundary. Grace was already regretting accepting the challenge but he held no fear of being bowled by a young lady, even one who put him in mind of Bessie.

Lawton held out his arm.

'Are you ready, Dr Grace?' he enquired.

'Quite ready, thank you, Bertie.'

'In that case … play.'

Grace settled into his familiar stance, right foot parallel to the crease, left foot pointing towards extra cover. Jessie, he noticed, looked nervous. It was understandable. He'd go easy on her – the challenge was for her to bowl him out; there was nothing to be gained from hitting her all around the ground. There were no fielders for a start, but either way he certainly did not wish to humiliate the girl.

She took three steps towards the wicket. Grace's left toes raised from the ground and his bat lifted. The ball looped high and came at him faster than he'd anticipated. It was well-pitched up and he killed it just in front of him before knocking it back along the ground to the bowler.

'Very nice, Miss Lawton,' he said.

'Thank you, Doctor.'

The second ball was slightly faster and flatter and pitched on leg stump. He patted it gently towards mid-on.

Jessie's third ball was looped higher again. He went forward with his front foot but the ball dipped, swerved very slightly, pitched on a good length, broke noticeably to off – and clipped the top of Grace's off stump.

A whoop went up from the gathering behind him, followed by applause. He looked at the pitch, then back at the stumps, his feet still planted as they had been when he'd played the shot. His cheeks reddened, a mix of anger and humiliation. Be gracious, Gilbert, he thought to himself. It's what his mother would have said, 'be gracious, Gilbert'. He would be gracious to Jessie, anyway, if not to Clement Edwards whose delight he could almost feel bouncing off the back of his neck.

'Well bowled, Miss Lawton, very well bowled indeed,' Edwards hooted. 'That one certainly had this old man well beaten.'

He didn't want to look behind him.

'And congratulations to you, Mr Edwards, you have your sovereign.'

'I assure you, Doctor,' came Edwards' laconic Welsh tones, 'I take no great pleasure from taking your money. And to prove it I suggest that we carry on. Double or quits says that Miss Lawton will bowl you out again in the remaining nine deliveries of our arrangement.'

Grace finally looked round.

'You are clearly an adventurous sportsman, Mr Edwards,' he said. 'We have made a great effort this morning to come here from the house so it would be a waste for the sake of just three balls. In the circumstances I am happy to accept those terms.'

He looked back up the wicket to where Jessie was standing a little awkwardly, holding the ball.

'Assuming Miss Lawton is happy to carry on?' he said.

'I would be delighted to continue bowling to you for as long as you wish to indulge me,' she said.

'In that case, we may continue when you are ready, Miss.'

He settled into his stance again. The fourth delivery was wide of the off stump and he hit the ball gently back to Jessie. The fifth was almost identical, with the same result. The next delivery was short of a length and broke towards leg: he was quickly on to the back foot and instinctively pulled the ball hard to square leg. Two small boys set off in pursuit. There was a smattering of applause.

'Apologies, Miss Lawton, my instincts rather got the better of me.'

'That's quite all right, Doctor, it was there to be hit and deserved no less.'

After a bout of pushing and a brief wrestle, the boys ran back from the outfield and handed the ball to Jessie.

Grace settled into his stance again. While he had hit the ball through instinct as much as anything else, there was, he had to admit to himself, a certain level of retribution in his mighty forearms as he sent the ball fizzing away to the long grass at the edge of the field.

Jessie took her three steps and sent down a high, arcing delivery. He watched it carefully; in the split second the ball was in the air he debated whether to block the ball or drive it back past Jessie. A defensive block would be best, he thought, and he stepped out to where the ball pitched. As he slid the bat along the ground to guard against a potential shooter, the ball bounced, higher than he'd anticipated, looped over the shoulder of his bat and knocked into the off stump. He clamped his eyes closed as he heard the bails hit the turf, followed almost immediately by a yell from Edwards and more warm applause. He opened his eyes and saw Jessie, her hands linked together in front of her, her eyes cast down at the ground. He could tell she was smiling and he couldn't blame her. But his main feeling was one of intense humiliation.

This time he made no attempt at platitude. He just made to walk back towards the house.

'Come now, Doctor.' It was Edwards' voice from behind him. To be fair to the man there was no sense of triumph or crowing in his voice.

'Come now, Doctor, don't leave us. May I propose that we continue with the final five balls? And again, shall we say double or quits? Four sovereigns, now, says Jessie will break your wicket once more.'

'As you wish, Mr Edwards,' replied Grace. 'But I assure you the bails could not be disturbed a third time, with all due respect to Miss Lawton.'

His first instinct had been to get away from the field as quickly as possible but it wasn't the lure of four sovereigns that persuaded him back. It was the realisation that this young woman really could bowl very well. Her technique was in fact very similar to his own. A short shuffle to the wicket, the arm barely rising above the level of the shoulder, the ball being given plenty of air, and not seeming to mind being hit to the boundary if it meant a wicket followed soon afterwards.

'Are you happy to continue, Miss Lawton?' called Edwards.

'I am quite happy as long as Dr Grace is happy,' said Jessie.

He replaced the bails, took a fresh guard from Bertie, and prepared to face Jessie again. Three balls came down the pitch, each of which he watched as carefully as if it were Alfred Shaw or Fred Spofforth sending them down. The first two were on a length on off stump and easily defended back to Jessie. The third was on middle and leg and he allowed it to hit him on the pad with the bat alongside to protect his stumps.

He wished he'd thought of this earlier. For one thing, after the events at Derby yesterday and the previous evening's conversation Bertie was never going to give him out leg before, and, for another, Jessie was clearly far too polite to appeal for lbw. Perhaps most importantly, the wager rested on her bowling him out: no other method of dismissal mattered. He knocked the ball back up the field, feeling satisfied that, for all the attendant humiliation he'd suffered, he would yet be relieving Mr Edwards of his four sovereigns after all.

'Two more to come, Bertie?'

'Two to come, Doctor.'

The next ball was again pitched towards middle and leg but this time was faster and with a slightly flatter trajectory. It pitched in front of him and he went to block it with his pad again. The ball skidded through low, hit the inside edge of his bat, then the heel of his boot and rolled back to hit the base of the middle stump. The bails fell almost apologetically.

He breathed in, a giant deep breath, and exhaled expansively. He dropped the bat on to the ground and stamped off back in the direction of the house, peeling off first one glove and throwing it to the turf and then the other. Nobody said a word. Everybody watched him go.

'I rather suspect lunch will be interesting,' said Bertie, pulling up the single stump in front of him at the bowler's end.

Thursday 2 March 1905

His vision swam and it felt as if the world had shuddered ever so slightly on its axis. The cable gave only the barest detail: that his eldest son Bertie, who shared his famous initials and worked as a schoolmaster on the Isle of Wight, had died on the operating table while having his appendix removed.

Agnes appeared at his side and all he could do was wordlessly hand her the piece of paper. She read it, dropped it to the floor, let out a wail, ran into the parlour and collapsed on to the chaise longue.

It couldn't be true. If Bertie had died he would have been there, as he was with Bessie. It couldn't happen like this, with a knock at the door and a piece of paper folded inside an envelope that had the power to shatter his and Agnes's world. It couldn't possibly happen like this. He sat down heavily on the stairs, reached out for the cable and read it again and again.

Poor Bertie had had a lot to live up to during his short life. He was as tall and lean as his father had been, but of a quieter, more circumspect nature. He'd been a keen cricketer – like his father he had a bat in his hand from an early age – but to W.G.'s frustration Bertie never looked remotely like emulating his own exploits on the

cricket field. He'd spent endless hours with him in the
nets, bowling ball after ball at him, but his eldest son
could never shake off the awkward, stiff aspect that
characterised his technique. He was still a more than
decent player, captaining his school, appearing for the
county and showing definite promise on going up to
Cambridge University, but it was clear that despite all
his father's encouragement he was never going to be
more than an average player at best.

There were flashes – he thought fondly of the large
stand they'd shared for MCC against the University in
1894 when Bertie made 50, and the time in 1901 when
Bertie and Billy Murdoch put on 355 for the first wicket
for London County – but even when selected for the
Varsity game he failed to shine: he was unspectacular in
1895 and bagged a pair in 1896.

The Old Man couldn't fathom why his son didn't
follow his own success on the cricket field. He was
from the same stock, after all, and had had the same
amount of coaching and opportunities from the
youngest of ages, yet he remained such an unexpressive,
almost mechanical player. In cricket terms, he lacked
personality; he batted as if by numbers. His father was
perplexed by it. Bertie still made him proud, of course –
W.G. had purchased his first frock coat and silk hat to
wear for the occasion of Bertie's first Varsity game,
which was also the first match at Lord's he'd ever
attended as a spectator, but he couldn't fathom why the

boy never followed in his footsteps. And now they would never play together again.

The news came as a dreadful shock. He knew an appendix removal was a serious operation but it was rarely fatal. They'd had no time to prepare for this: in his head Bertie was still that tall, serious, bespectacled boy who could come down the stairs at any moment, pushing his glasses up his nose as he seemed to do every two minutes. While Bessie's demise had been hellish and a vicious hand for the fates to play, at least the nature of her illness had allowed them to prepare to some extent for the end. But this – a telegram, out of the blue to follow up the one they'd received two days earlier announcing his sudden illness – this was no way to learn of the death of an eldest son.

While Annie consoled Agnes in the parlour he shut himself away in his study and sat at his desk, and only then allowed the tears to come. First Bessie, now Bertie. Half the Grace brood gone before they'd had a chance truly to flourish.

Encouraging and proud of his son as he was, and of course he loved the boy, sitting there in his study staring at the desk he reflected upon how they'd never been particularly close. From early childhood Bertie had been studious, quiet and reserved, almost exactly the opposite of his father, and other than cricket little had bound them together beyond biology. He was the antithesis of Bessie, who was so outgoing, opinionated and vivacious, but he supposed that, for all the assistance he'd given him, the strings he'd pulled, the encouragement he'd expressed, ultimately the boy had to find his own way and Bertie had chosen teaching, first at Oundle and then at the Royal Naval College on the Isle of Wight. With Bertie having lived away for so long and cricket keeping his father away from home for days at a time when he'd been a boy, the Old Man felt as though death had cheated him again.

The tears kept rolling and there was a pain in his soul. He tried to remember details, any details, of the stand they'd shared at Lord's, but all he could recall was the pair of them walking off the ground together, the Doctor having to take Bertie by the arm because he was, as always, lagging behind him.

Tuesday 5 September 1905

'It's been a poor show, all right, Harry.'

The greatest cricketer of them all sat in the bar of the Bournemouth Grand Hotel with its owner, Harry Preston, and lamented the state of the game. The second day had ended with the Gentlemen of the South bowled out for 217 in reply to the Players of the South's first innings total of 496. An incredible onslaught by Hampshire's South African all-rounder Charles Llewellyn had taken the Players' total from 299 for seven to just shy of 500. For a batsman to go in at number eight and score 186 had impressed even the Old Man as from point he watched the ball being sent to all corners of the ground. The Gentlemen's reply had never found its rhythm and he'd top-scored with just 43. The Gentleman would begin the day tomorrow by commencing the follow on.

'Certainly a little different from the Australia game, Doctor,' replied Preston.

A few days earlier Grace had led an England XI against the visiting Australian touring side also in Bournemouth and, despite fielding a makeshift team (Llewellyn played for the English side despite being

South African), lost a thrilling game by only one wicket against a team that included Clem Hill, Warwick Armstrong and Victor Trumper.

'Very different, Harry,' said Grace, thoughtfully. 'Very different indeed. I am also leading a very different side here.'

'Do you think you can bat all day tomorrow?' asked Preston.

'I doubt it very much. I just don't think we have the depth in the batting. It won't be much of a spectacle for you, I'm afraid, even if we make it as far as the final session.'

'Oh, I shan't be there for most of it,' said Preston, 'I'm motoring over to my hotel in Brighton tomorrow. My wife's been holding the fort there while I've been attending to you here.'

'Motoring, you say?'

W.G. stroked his beard. He had never travelled in a motor car.

'Oh yes, didn't I tell you? I have a four-cylinder De Dion-Bouton in which I travel between here and Brighton. It's a wonderful thing.'

'I don't doubt it, Harry, I don't doubt it. Brighton, you say?'

'Yes, I have the Royal York Hotel there, right by the Palace Pier.'

The Old Man continued stroking his beard.

'How long does it take you to drive as far as Brighton?'

'On a good day around four hours; a little less if I'm lucky with the level crossings and the floating bridge at Southampton.'

The beard stroking picked up speed.

'I have a game in Hastings beginning the day after tomorrow,' he said. 'Why don't I come with you in your motor car as far as Brighton?'

Preston thought for a moment.

'You'd be most welcome, Doctor,' he said, 'and of course I'd be able to put you up at the hotel tomorrow evening as my guest before your onward journey to Hastings, but I don't see how it can be possible.'

'Why not?'

'Well, you have a day's cricket to play tomorrow and I need to be in Brighton around four o'clock so will be leaving no later than noon.'

'No later than noon, you say. Very well, be at the ground at 11am sharp tomorrow.'

'But …'

'You have my word, Harry, that I will be seated in your Gideon Mutton or whatever it's called ready to depart for Brighton no later than noon tomorrow.'

The Old Man heaved himself out of his chair and offered Preston his hand.

'Goodnight, Harry. I am off to sleep soundly in one of your comfortable beds ahead of my first ever ride in a motor car tomorrow. I am looking forward to it very much.'

'Goodnight, Doctor,' said Preston, 'see you there at eleven sharp.'

The next morning Preston arrived at the ground in his car on the stroke of eleven o'clock to find no cricket played after an earlier rain shower had delayed the start. Grace bustled over to meet him.

'Harry, my dear chap,' he beamed. 'The start of play has been delayed very slightly but I still intend to ride with you to Brighton.'

Preston pulled out his watch and reminded the Champion that he intended to leave at noon.

'And I intend to be with you in your contraption when you do,' said Grace, just as the rain began to fall again.

Three hours passed, punctuated by showers that set the start of play back further each time. Preston resigned himself to the fact that they would leave when W.G. was ready and not before. Grace knew what Preston knew – that having W.G. Grace as a passenger in his car for a journey between two of his hotels was too great an opportunity to miss for the sake of a stern look from his wife when he arrived.

Finally, at 2.30 p.m., Grace strode out to open the innings with Hampshire's Charles Robson, having assured Preston they would be in Brighton before the day was out. The Old Man played the first over carefully, not scoring any runs and by the fourth over the score had reached seven with Grace still on nought. The first ball of Ted Dennett's next over was slightly overpitched on off stump and the old craftsman drove it emphatically to long-on for four. The crowd murmured its approval and applauded warmly. This was what they'd come to see. The second ball was on a good length and not particularly dangerous, but to the stunned amazement of the crowd the Champion patted a simple catch back to the bowler, who clutched the ball to his chest and looked around as if he couldn't quite believe what had just happened. Grace was already on his way back to the pavilion, head down, bat under arm, gloves coming off, almost before Dennett had taken the catch. As he strode off he caught sight of Preston.

'Terrible luck, Harry,' he called out. 'The ball must have hit a loose piece of earth and popped up. Still, on the bright side, at least I'll be able to join you on the run to Brighton. I shall be with you presently.'

And with that he disappeared into the pavilion. Preston was pleased: there was no greater publicist in the hotel business than he, and shuttling arguably the most recognisable person in the land between his hotels in his new automobile, well, you couldn't put a price on that kind of exposure, but he did feel a pang of guilt that the wily old goat had rather pulled a fast one on the crowd who had in the most part turned up to see him bat. At least he'd hit one ball to the boundary before lobbing up that dolly to Dennett, but otherwise, well, there were a few sixpences in the gateman's tray whose erstwhile owners may have been rueing their parting.

Ten minutes later the Doctor appeared, changed into his grey worsted suit and matching cap, carrying his cricket bag in one hand and his travelling bag in the other. He was grinning.

'See, Harry?' he said quietly as he placed his luggage in the back of the car. 'Told you I'd be ready.'

Preston took out his watch, looked at it, looked at his passenger, raised an eyebrow, opened the little door to the passenger seat and the Old Man hauled himself up on to the step.

'You're definitely not staying to see the match through to its conclusion, Doctor?' asked Preston knowingly, as Grace's considerable backside hovered in front of his face.

'These lads will manage fine without me, Harry,' he said as he settled into the passenger seat. 'There's not much I can do from the pavilion. And, anyway, Charlie Fry is there and there's no better man to leave in charge of things than him.'

Preston cranked the handle at the front of the car and the engine spluttered into life. The Old Man gripped the door with both hands, a little unsettled by the vibrations and the noise. Preston hopped up into the driver's seat.

'Don't worry, Doctor,' he said over the sound of the engine, 'it's perfectly safe.'

He wrenched the car into gear, grasped the steering wheel with both hands and eased the vehicle into motion. It lurched slightly, and Grace found himself rocking back and forth in his seat. It was an unnerving sensation: he was high up on the vehicle, it was open and a long way from the ground. Used to either trains or cabs, he felt that being in motion like this he should either be enclosed in a carriage or at the very least regarding the rear ends of a couple of sturdy horses clopping away wearily in front of him.

'What do you think, Doctor?' said Preston as the car pulled out of the cricket ground and on to the main road. He didn't answer. He couldn't answer: he didn't know how he felt yet, this was unlike anything he had ever experienced before.

As they chugged out of Bournemouth and into the New Forest, however, he started to relax and enjoy himself.

'This is a fine way to travel, Harry!' he said eventually over the noise of the engine, clamping his hat to his head in order to stop it blowing away.

'It's the future, Doctor!' came the reply.

After a journey of around four hours the car pulled on to Brighton seafront, headed towards the Palace Pier and parked outside the entrance of the Royal York Hotel bathed in evening sunshine. The engine died but it took the Old Man a while for his ears to adjust to the absence of engine noise. His face felt flushed from the wind and his rear end ached from being seated on a thin cushion for hours on end but he had found the journey intriguingly enjoyable.

Preston helped him down from the passenger seat and the Old Man stepped back to look at the car. It still appeared outlandish to him, as if it was somehow incomplete. It looked wrong without horses in front: to think that all the power of propulsion came from in that little box at the front. With its curves and plush upholstery, noisy engine and sturdy chassis, it was a strange hybrid of elegance and function. This was really the future? He pursed his lips doubtfully, retrieved his bags from the rear of the car and waited for Preston to show him to his room.

'Did you enjoy the ride then, Doctor?' he asked.

'Very much, Harry, thank you,' said Grace. 'I would certainly like to ride with you again sometime.'

Later that evening, after dinner, he stepped out to take the sea air. Having crossed the road and descended the steps to the beach, he mashed his way across the pebbles until he reached the lapping waves gently washing the stones in front of him. Aside from the chain of lights strung along the Palace Pier all was dark from the water shifting in front of him to the beach that stretched out either side of him to the sky. But for a few wispy clouds the night was clear and the stars were spread above him in a beautiful canopy. Such opportunities for solitude had always been rare, but then he'd never really cared much for solitude. It was probably this rare opportunity to be alone with his thoughts that made him think of Arthur Shrewsbury. How he could have done with Arthur today rather than the raggle-taggle eleven he'd scraped together for the game at Bournemouth. Arthur would have made the difference; his was always the first name that came to mind whenever he was asked to put a team together. There was no finer batsman on a sticky wicket than Arthur, and his 164 for England in 1886 against Australia with Spofforth in full cry would last long in the memory of all who saw it. Even the Champion himself had to admit that Shrewsbury was probably the finest batsman in the land for a time during the eighties.

It was two years now since poor Arthur took his own life. It didn't seem like it. At the end of the 1902 season he'd complained of kidney pains and had spent an uncomfortable winter, barely able to walk at times, Grace had heard. Yet a stream of doctors could find nothing wrong with him: even a London specialist to whom he'd made a special journey in February couldn't diagnose the problem. It was then that Shrewsbury realised there was little chance of him playing serious cricket in the coming season.

On 22 May he'd gone into Jackson's gunsmiths in Nottingham and bought a revolver and some ammunition. A week later he'd returned, complaining he couldn't load the weapon and learned he'd bought the wrong bullets. The shop exchanged them for the correct ones and he'd gone home to his lodgings where his lady friend Gertrude was waiting, concerned about his mood. That afternoon he'd said to her, 'I shall be in the churchyard before many more days are up', and she'd scolded him for talking in such a way.

He seemed to have cheered up a little by the evening and when he sent Gertrude downstairs to make him a cup of cocoa she thought he'd come out of his funk. While in the kitchen she heard a loud noise from upstairs. She went into the hallway and called up to him, asking what had happened.

'Nothing,' was the response and she returned to the kitchen. Seconds later there was another loud report and when Gertrude rushed upstairs she found Shrewsbury in bed, insensible, having first shot himself in the chest and then in the temple. She ran for the doctor but by the time he arrived Shrewsbury was dead.

The inquest recorded the verdict as suicide brought on by the belief that he was suffering from a serious illness even though the coroner could find absolutely nothing physically wrong with him.

The Old Man stood in the darkness by the sea and tried to imagine what might have been going through Arthur's mind. The realisation that he wouldn't be playing much in the way of cricket that season must have been a terrible blow. Having soldiered through the winter suffering from these crippling pains, the thought of the coming sun-blessed days on the cricket field must have been the only thing keeping the old boy going, he thought. When that was taken away from him he just couldn't face the prospect of a life of constant pain, but mostly he couldn't face the prospect of a life without 'the moment', that beautiful, exultant time when the ball left the bowler's hand on its way to you and nothing else mattered.

He felt a fleeting pang of guilt. Today he had deliberately thrown away his wicket in order to join Harry Preston in his motor car. Today he had taken the game for granted, the game that could conceivably have saved Arthur's life. Arthur would have given anything to have been at that wicket today.

There was still a good deal of batting left in Arthur Shrewsbury, he mused. If he could have just got past that evening when it seemed that all was futile and lost, he could even have been down here on the south coast with him, looking forward to the Hastings Festival and talking about what kind of wicket it might be.

Standing there alone, as a few drops of rain began to fall, he could almost sense Arthur next to him, in cricket whites and dark blue blazer, hands in his trouser pockets.

'A sticky one tomorrow, I'd say, Gilbert,' he half heard. 'I think I should like to open.'

He looked back up at the stars and relished for a minute how small they made him feel, how insignificant, then turned his back on the sea and crunched back up the beach towards the bright lights of the hotel.

Tuesday 18 July 1906

As soon as the ball came off the bat he let out a frustrated, strangled yelp. It had kept lower than he'd anticipated and come off the bottom of the blade. If he'd middled it, it would have ended up comfortably in the crowd. This wasn't his bat, it was George Beldam's, and while he'd admired it every time he'd seen it and had been anxious to get his hands on it, on this occasion craftsmanship alone couldn't help him. The ball went in a curving arc towards Albert Trott at mid-off who took a comfortable catch. He looked across at the scoreboard: he'd made 74, a pretty decent effort all told. As he tucked his bat under his arm and pulled off his gloves the applause began to ring out as the Oval crowd stood as one. He was, he had to admit, exhausted. He'd set out to score at least 58, a run for each year of his life, and had passed that figure comfortably, but the last 20 runs or so had been hard, physically hard.

He'd been through his reference books and notes and calculated that this was his 85th Gentlemen v Players match, 41 years after his first. This, the final day of the game, was also his 58th birthday which, everyone suspected, was the reason why he had been invited to captain the Gentlemen after an absence from the fixture of two years.

As he dragged his enormous frame back towards the pavilion, a walk he'd made many times, usually against his will, he realised that he was actually looking forward to getting off the field. His footsteps were heavier than usual but the disappointment of getting out, especially to a mistimed shot, was, he realised, tinged with a sense of relief. His feet were sore and his legs almost trembled with tiredness: running between the wickets was becoming a real problem for him now. In fact, he wasn't even 'running' as such any more; it was more of a lumber, a glorified hobble.

When he stood at the wicket and took his stance he still felt as he did 40 years ago or more: that he was ready for anything and could achieve anything he desired. That familiar settling of the body, right foot behind and parallel with the crease, the left foot pointing slightly outwards towards the bowler, the bottom of his bat resting gently against the little toe of his right foot. Head upright, perfectly straight, looking down the wicket. As the bowler approached the crease he'd lift the ball of his left foot, leaving his heel on the ground, pick up the bat right over middle stump, feint as if he was briefly going to play a stroke as the ball left the bowler's hand, and, when the ball was in the air, the exultant moment arrived when he truly felt ageless. That half a second or whatever it might be between the ball leaving the bowler's hand and reaching him was the moment he still lived for. It was why he was still, even approaching

60, prepared to make long, uncomfortable train journeys to all parts of the country, put up with lumpy hotel beds, scan the newspapers and the skies for clues of approaching weather, climb rickety stairs to change in damp, draughty dressing-rooms, pull boots on to his gnarled old feet and walk out, bat in hand, on to whatever ground it happened to be that day. That moment, when it was just him and the ball, the ultimate, simplest duel, reading the trajectory, duetting with physics, watching for the spin, deducing whether to play forward or back, attack or defend, *that's* what made everything worthwhile. The repeated, metronomic task of ball pitted against bat, when the rest of the world melted away, the aches of old age, the responsibilities of captaincy, the concerns for the make-up of the team, the machinations of committees, everything left his mind the moment that ball left the bowler's hand. Then it was just the lightning calculations of his mind, the translation of those calculations into a decision, the transmission of that decision to his body, limbs, feet and hands and then the outcome of the decision, whether it be killing the ball stone dead with impenetrable defence, or sending it skimming away across the grass with a stroke timed so perfectly that he felt no vibrations in his hands.

That moment, that repetitive, relentless, ritual of duelling, that was why he was still here, 58 years old, playing in one of the greatest matches in modern sport.

This time he felt the vibrations in his arms – a curse on that crack in the pitch that had stopped him timing the shot right – as well as the aches in his feet and legs. He'd experienced that timeless, ageless moment of weightlessness and the complete mental mastery of his body for the last time in a Gentlemen v Players match.

He approached the gate, acknowledging the tremendous ovation of the Oval crowd, and wearily climbed the steps, making his way to the dressing-room. He walked in, swung Beldam's bat, dropped it on to the table and announced, 'There, I shan't play any more.'

With that he sat down heavily on a bench under the peg from which his clothes hung while his team-mates filed past one by one, congratulating him, shaking his hand, slapping his shoulders and wishing him well.

Finally he unbuckled his pads, kicked off his boots, placed his hands either side of him on the bench and looked down at his cricket bag. He closed his eyes and imagined himself back out there, the ball about to be bowled, to release him into the moment when such mortal concerns as age and weariness melt away to nothing.

Monday 20 April 1908

He pulled his thick, long-sleeved sweater over his head and unfurled it down his body until the heavy hem hung by his thighs. Stepping on to the balcony, he was hit by a wind cold enough to make him catch his breath, something that certainly didn't improve the view. Where he was used to looking out across a sun-kissed Oval, the benches packed with boater-topped spectators, today there was barely a smattering of people in heavy coats and caps beneath grey scudding clouds. Even the grass, normally a verdant green, looked blue-grey.

'What a day this is for cricket,' he said as he surveyed the grim scene.

The wind had begun in the Arctic, nature's icicle-breath knifing its icy way across the fjords of Norway, picking up pace over the dark, white-tipped waters of the North Sea, skittering across the Fens and the flatlands of Norfolk and Suffolk and channelling itself up the Thames Estuary, skimming the gas holders and swooping across the Oval pitch to ruffle a long, greying beard. Its owner hunched his shoulders and thrust his hands deep into the pockets of his cricket whites.

He turned back inside the dressing-room where the rest of the Gentlemen of England were arranging heavy sweaters on laps and dancing with the long sleeves as they readied themselves to pull them over their heads.

'The summer game, eh, Doc?' came a voice from somewhere beneath a thick layer of cable-knit, and everyone laughed.

'I apologise, gentlemen, for losing the toss,' he announced turning back to the room. 'I am certain Surrey only chose to bat in order that the rest of their eleven could stay sitting around the fire.'

There was a ripple of laughter but he wasn't entirely sure whether he was joking or not.

He looked back out of the window and estimated there were barely 1,500 spectators out there. In all his years in the game The Oval had never presented such a bleak prospect at the start of a match.

At the same time he was aware this was most likely to be his last ever first-class match. He was leading what was essentially a London County side facing their customary season opener against Surrey, but as the London County club had long lost its status they had become the Gentlemen of England in order to keep the fixture first class. Even with the heavy and committed involvement of the greatest cricketer in the land, the failure of London County to be admitted to the County Championship and the inexplicable lack of consistent support from the local suburban population ensured that the club was in the process of easing its way into oblivion.

In three months he'd turn 60. Sixty! In his mind he felt as young as ever. Even his 50th seemed only a couple of years ago but where first the years, now the decades were flitting by like never before. For as long as he remembered he'd mapped his life in cricket seasons, commencing net practice as early as the weather would allow and then spending almost every day until the Scarborough Festival in September either playing or travelling to and from matches. The last three or four years had seen a gradual reduction in his playing commitments but he still woke early on a match day, the excitement in his stomach the same as it had been when he was a child. Agnes commented each spring how his eyes would regain their sparkle when he came down for breakfast on those early season match days.

It had been the same that morning, the first match morning of the season. Even a glance out of the window to see the trees being whipped back and forth by the wind and hearing the smack of sleet against the windows couldn't dim the flame of excitement that heralded the start of another season.

'Gilbert, you're definitely at your happiest when there's a cricket bag packed and ready by the front door,' Agnes had said, looping a strand of hair back over his ear and brushing his cheek with the back of her hand as he set about his plate of eggs.

He looked back from the window at his team and rubbed his hands on the front of his sweater.

'Right, gentlemen, there's a match to be played. Out we go.'

He led the team down through the pavilion and out of the door on to the ground. The strong wind boomed immediately in his ears, caused an involuntary intake of breath and picked and plucked at the heavy old sweater as it tried to find a way in to freeze those old bones. His legs felt stiff, his fingertips and the palms of his hands thrummed and stung as he caught the ball they tossed between them. He hated the soft hands of a new season: with the reduced amount of cricket he was playing now it took even longer for his palms to toughen up.

He arranged his field and as he took his customary position at point he heard a ghost of applause being whipped away in the wind as the Surrey openers Hobbs and Marshal walked to the wicket. Barely four weeks earlier Hobbs had been playing for the touring England side in 97° against Western Australia at Perth – this was something quite different. It was possibly no surprise therefore that Brearley's third ball of the game knocked his middle stump clean out of the ground.

Half an hour later thick flakes of snow began to blow across the field, billowing out of a featureless grey sky and giving the umpires little choice but to suspend play. The teams scuttled off to the relative warmth of the dressing-rooms where flames were roaring in the grates and, most welcomingly, under the tea urn.

Within the hour the players were trooping back out again as a faint dusting of snow lay on the outfield. A few spectators had given up and gone home already, but as the day progressed the weather improved and there was even some sunshine in the afternoon. The bitter wind from the north-east didn't abate, however, and for once Grace wasn't sorry to leave the field at the end of the day, with Surrey 381 for eight.

The following morning was brighter, but still cold. The Gentlemen wrapped up the Surrey innings for 390 within 15 minutes of the start, meaning Grace opened with Henry Keigwin in poor light with practically the entire day ahead of them. He lost his partner almost immediately for a duck but Grace dug in, defending solidly, the way he dragged the bottom of the bat along the pitch towards the ball a legacy of the terrible pitches of the sixties and seventies where shooters were rife. When rain began to fall half an hour into the innings, causing another break in play, he'd scored just four of the Gentlemen's 21 for the loss of three wickets.

In all he'd spend an hour and a half at the crease for 15 runs when he was clean bowled by Sydney Busher, a pace bowler who'd made his name with Barnes Cricket Club and could make the ball break off the wicket to great effect. Busher whooped with the delight of a player who had just claimed W.G. Grace as the first wicket of his first-class career.

The Gentlemen were all out for 219 shortly after 5 p.m. when the umpires, no doubt chilled to the bone from standing still in the freezing wind all afternoon, called an end to the day's play in gloomy light, with the Crawford brothers the only batsmen to pass 20 but contributing more than 150 – without them the total would have been utterly embarrassing.

Surrey invited the Gentlemen to follow on the next morning and Grace again walked out to open the innings with Keigwin for his last ever knock in a first-class game. The contrasting pair, the rotund, grey-bearded old man who moved slowly and heavily between the wickets and the wiry, nimble-footed Essex youngster, proved resistant to the Surrey bowling, but even in such an apparently lost cause it was the Old Man who took the fight to the bowlers. After his stonewalling of the first innings he played his old, natural game, relishing the treatment of each delivery on its merits, blocking and cutting, pulling and driving. It may have been cold, it may have been April, there may have been barely a couple of hundred spectators in the ground and he may have been feeling the aches in his cold bones of a man in his 60th year, but he was still relishing the moment, the moment when the ball was released and age and the match and the cold and the empty enclosures didn't matter a jot. If it was pitched up he'd drive it, if it was short he'd pull or cut and, sure enough, boundaries came.

The Times the next day would praise his attacking shots, calling them an 'object lesson to any young player', but the fun was not to last. When he'd scored 25 he again lost his middle stump to a ball from Busher that broke sharply off the pitch and that was it. He strode back to the pavilion tapping the toe of his bat on the ground as he went. He stood tall, his back straight, dignified and awesome. The smattering of people in the ground applauded as loudly as they could, trying to make it sound as if they were a multitude, thinking about how they could tell their grandchildren of the day they'd seen the Champion batting at The Oval and for a while it had been like watching him in his prime, the timing, the power, the presence. And when he'd walked off, even though the famous beard may have been streaked with grey and the old MCC cap hung like a battered rag on his head, he'd left that field like a god, as if he carried the entire game of cricket with him. They'd tell of how everyone there forgot about the cold and the reduced circumstances and were instead transported back to the golden summer days of a golden age.

In a few moments the Old Man had walked through the Gentlemen's gate and disappeared into the pavilion and everything was dreary again.

He was quiet as he changed, remaining in the dressing-room as the wickets fell quickly. The Gentlemen of England – such a grand name for a scratch team of journeymen cricketers whistled up by hook or by crook – were all out just before lunch for 130, losing the match heavily by an innings and 41 runs.

The two teams took their lunch and then the players began to disperse, all brief handshakes and terse farewells spoken through pipe-clenched teeth and the echoing creaks of footsteps descending the wooden staircase until there was just the Old Man left, cricket bag packed and strapped, overcoat on and dark eyes looking out from beneath his hat.

He sat in the dressing-room, the last man, looking at the wall opposite for a while, curiously reluctant to depart. This, he knew, was the end of his first-class career. He'd scored more than fifty thousand runs and taken nearly three thousand wickets – he still kept meticulous records at home – but those totals now would be static for ever. Those figures as they stood today, from the moment his middle stump went over that morning, would stand now for eternity.

He stood up and walked towards the balcony. The wind tried to yank the door closed when he grasped the handle and pulled, but he was soon outside, beard teased by the gusts, sitting looking across the empty ground. The cloud had dropped into mist and The Oval was framed by a wispy halo, sepia-tinged by the smoke of a thousand chimneys, the gas holders looming in the murk.

All was still and silent. He sat for a while watching his breath clouds whisked up to the heavens and looked down to the empty pitch, on which barely a couple of hours earlier he'd been driving and pulling and cutting, utterly lost in the moment. There was something sad about a recently emptied cricket ground, he reflected. The beer bottles and peanut shells were pushed around beneath the benches by the wind, the echoes of the crowd had long dissipated, the sound of bat on ball risen to heaven. The empty Oval was like an old ship, dignified and noble, abandoned in a dry dock, all its adventures and stories and personalities soaked into the rivets, the plating, the carved oak interiors. He could see the scars on the wicket from the match just completed and in his mind's eye he saw that ball from Busher, breaking off the pitch past the shoulder of his bat as he dragged it forward, and hitting middle stump. The dreaded click of ball striking stump and the hollow woody thump of stump striking ground echoed inside his head. He wasn't replaying it for the purposes of revising technique, he wasn't wondering what he could have done differently – nothing, was the answer, he'd have played exactly the same shot – but it was the appreciation that that ball was the last he'd ever face in first-class cricket.

He closed his eyes and it was as if the years opened beneath him to fall back to a sunny July day in 1880. He'd made 152 in the first innings of his first Test against the Australians, racing to 91 for the first wicket with E.M., but it wasn't his own achievements that had come into his mind, it was what happened the following day. Fred Morley had got well among the Australian order and when big George Bonnor came in at seven with those mighty forearms they were 80-odd for five in reply to 420. Lord Harris threw the ball to Alfred Shaw at the Vauxhall End because it was clear Bonnor was looking to make some big hits and Shaw was wily enough to coax him into a mistake. Sure enough, within a few balls he caught hold of a ball from Shaw that dipped slightly at the last moment and sent it steepling into the air towards the cover boundary. From point the Old Man had a perfect view of its enormous parabola; so high did it climb that the batsmen were able to complete two runs. If it hadn't been for that late dip of Shaw's, thought Grace, the ball could have ended up on the roof of Waterloo railway station. He looked down from the ball to see, racing around the boundary, eyes not leaving the ball, setting himself beneath it, dear brother Fred. Grace watched as that handsomely youthful face upturned, eyes on the ball and, smack, the ball dropped into his hands with minimal fuss and was clutched to his chest. Fred was the finest fielder of all the Graces but that catch was outstanding even for him. W.G. had roared his approval along with the crowd. The memory of the childlike delight in Fred's eyes, that same sparkle that Bessie always had in hers, was as fresh in his mind as yesterday even though nearly 30 years had passed since. With the crowd's cheers and hurrahs, the congratulations of his team-mates washing over him, he'd never seen Fred so happy, so vibrant, so thrumming with life.

Yet within two weeks they were burying him. A few days after the Test he'd caught a cold but none the less travelled from Bristol to Stroud to play for the United South. He made runs, too, but a couple of soakings during the game only made his cold worse. From Stroud he'd set off for Winchester where he was due to play his next match, a benefit, one he really didn't want to miss. Staying at a hotel in Basingstoke en route, his symptoms worsened to pneumonia and he was confined to his bed there. He rallied, declined, rallied and declined until finally he died peacefully at lunchtime on the afternoon of 22 September. W.G. and his father had received the news at the little railway station at Bradford-on-Avon while waiting for a train to take them to see him.

He'd always blamed himself for not being there. Dr Charles Frere Webb was an old family friend who lived in the town and had attended to Fred for the whole week. Their cousin Walter Gilbert had travelled up, too, and the prognoses arriving from them both suggested that there was no call for despair. Neither of them would have concealed the gravity of the situation and his terminal decline was sudden and shattering, yet, having received the terrible news in the afternoon shade of a sleepy rural railway station, he still felt he should have gone to Basingstoke and attended to his brother when he was first taken ill. It was 28 years ago now – Fred had been 29 so had now been dead almost as long as he'd been alive – but the memories of that catch, his face and his eyes, and the terrible vision of the station master at Bradford-on-Avon rushing up to them on the platform, the expression on his face almost obviating the need to read the telegram, were as fresh as yesterday. He could even remember the jingle of the man's keys as he ran along the platform calling out to them and waving the telegram as they prepared to board the train.

He looked out across the field to where Fred had taken that extraordinary catch. The contrast between that joyous, sun-blessed moment in front of a Test match crowd and the bare, soulless, sleet-strafed view in front of him couldn't have been more marked; couldn't have illustrated better that thin line between joyous life and pitiless death.

The thought of a life without a cricket match to look forward to made him shudder, so it was a thought he tended to banish whenever it arose. But how much longer could he go on? He'd proved in this sad husk of a game that he could still play his shots all around the wicket against first-class bowlers despite his advancing years and increasing aches and pains. The desire was still there, the childlike enthusiasm, the longing for the moment when nothing else mattered and there was nothing else in the world. He couldn't imagine a life without that. Couldn't countenance it. That, he thought, truly would be hell.

Would he ever walk out at The Oval again? Was this game, this dreadful game in the cold and the snow in front of a handful of spectators, to be his swansong here?

After all the great occasions? The triumphs and the disappointments? That epic Test of 1882 when the Australians came here and won in one of the most thrilling final days he could remember? That dramatic, tension-filled final day when England, needing only 85 to win, were bowled out for 77, Spofforth running through the order with speed, guile and fearsome determination?

They say Spofforth was fired up that day after he, Grace, had run out Jones the previous day. Certainly when Grace walked to the wicket to bat on the final day Bonnor and Garrett had made it disgracefully plain that they felt he had acted improperly. Yet W.G. felt entirely vindicated in running out Jones. The man had completed a run, Grace had the ball in his hand and the batsman had left the crease to pat down a divot. The ball, as far as he was concerned and, importantly, as far as the umpires and therefore the laws of the game were concerned, was live so there was no question Grace wouldn't knock off a bail and make an entirely justifiable appeal.

The innings he played that last day, among all the tension, the histrionics of the Australians, the extraordinarily good bowling of Spofforth, the enormous crowd sharing the unbearable tension – he'd heard that as the game edged towards a conclusion one man bit clean through the wooden handle of his umbrella and another dropped down dead from the anxiety – was one of his finest, despite it being in vain and the Australians claiming their first ever Test victory in this country. He'd guided them to 51 for three before he hit Boyle to mid-off and was caught for 35, easily the top score in what turned out to be a losing cause. Of course he hated losing, especially to the Australians and especially after the insults of Bonnor and Garrett, but that innings was one of the most satisfactorily defiant of his life. He looked out at the field and could see Spofforth running in from the Vauxhall End, one of the hundreds of ghosts of players he'd battled with and against out there over the years.

There were footsteps on the stairs, the jingle of a set of keys and the creak of the dressing-room door opening behind him. A head poked out of the balcony door.

'Oh, I'm sorry, Doctor, I didn't think there was anyone still here,' said George, the caretaker. 'I was about to lock up.'

'It's all right, George,' he replied. 'I was just going.'

He heaved himself to his feet.

'A rum time of year for a game of cricket, Doctor,' said George. 'It was perishing. You must have been feeling it in your bones.'

'I was indeed, George,' he replied. 'Feeling it in my bones.'

Saturday 24 April 1909

Curiosity. That's mainly what had compelled him to attend the 1909 Football Association Cup Final at the Crystal Palace. That and the fact his old local team Bristol City had reached the final for the first time in its history. The same was true of their opponents, Manchester United from the North-West. As the final was being played practically on his Sydenham doorstep, meaning he could be back home in front of the fire with a whisky and soda within 20 minutes of the final whistle, he was delighted to accept an invitation to attend as an honoured guest.

Grace may have been a cricket man, but he appreciated all sports. He still went out beagling with the Worcester Park hounds whenever he could and still thoroughly enjoyed crown green bowls, a more genteel version of the West Country skittles of his childhood. Indeed it was a sport at which he excelled to the extent of captaining England in its first bowls international in 1903, winning the first home international tournament (even if he did have to point out the quirk of the rules that gave the title to England rather than the much-fancied Scots and insist it was upheld). He liked nothing more than sending his wood thundering down the green to scatter his opponents' far and wide, in spite of the frequent whispers about the tactical value of his unsubtle philosophy. The number of Scots in his 'England' team was also a subject of discussion, out of his earshot.

In addition he'd discovered the pleasures of curling while in Scotland for bowls and still played whenever he could find a game at an ice rink, usually at the Princes' Rink in Kensington but sometimes travelling as far as Maidenhead.

He was a lusty wielder of a golf club, too. Again his style was straightforward: he loved to belt the ball down the fairway and, now he had a putting green in the back garden, the more intricate wiles of the game were opening up to him as well. And, of course, no sociable evening was complete without at least an hour or two around the billiard table.

It was generally as a participant that he enjoyed his sport: like most career sportsmen he was a reluctant, nay, terrible spectator, but the sense of occasion attracted him to the Cup Final as much as its locality. Association football was still a strange concept to him. He'd never played the game but had become increasingly aware of the sport's growing popularity, particularly among the working classes. Often in his general practice days when he'd attend at the house of a poor family, on the occasions when cricket talk had been exhausted the man of the house would try to engage him about the current fortunes of Bristol City or Rovers and so he had always kept a cursory eye on their progress. With their Saturday afternoons free for leisure, the men would head in droves to Ashton Gate or Eastville, pay a shilling and watch the brief, 90-minute skirmish between two teams and then dissect the afternoon's events into the evening in the pubs across the town.

So, while curious, he was also concerned that the association game was eclipsing cricket as the spectator sport of the masses. As he left the house in Laurel Park Road well in advance of kick-off, the sight of streams of men in flat caps and three-piece suits wearing the favours of both sides seemed only to confirm his fears. Some wore elaborate rosettes, others enormous top hats lined with coloured crêpe paper. It looked as much a carnival as a sporting occasion.

He walked among them towards the football ground, cheerily acknowledging the greetings and ribbing of the supporters. 'This ball will be a bit too large for you, Doctor!' they cried. 'If you wonder where the middle stumps are, they're goals at each end!' and the more direct, 'Thy team's in for a beatin' today, W.G.!'

He fell into conversation with a group of men who'd travelled from Salford and was astounded to hear they had journeyed overnight on a special train that had offloaded them at King's Cross at three o'clock in the morning into a heavy downpour. They'd sheltered as they could until daylight, warmed themselves in a tearoom as soon as it had opened, wiping the steamed-up windows and gazing out at the dark, rainy streets of London, the cold still in their feet, their clothes and their bones as they cradled chipped cups of steaming tea. They'd seen as many London sights as they could – 'we hoped thon Houses of Parliament might keep us warm what with all th'hot air gets spoke in there' – and then made their way down to the Crystal Palace for the match.

The Old Man had never seen such dedication. Granted this was the football season's showpiece occasion but, even so, he'd never heard of anything approaching such mass spectator devotion in the cricket world and he couldn't fathom why.

Across the park they streamed in their thousands, long lines of boisterous, flat-capped chattering humanity. While he could pick out Bristolian accents among the throng, it was clear that the supporters from Manchester would significantly outnumber those from the west.

At length he reached the VIP entrance, was shown up the steps at the back of the grandstand and made his way to a seat in the pavilion, set back from the touchline and flanked at angles by stands on either side. He was presented with a programme, found his seat and was astonished at the numbers already filling the ground – the bank on the opposite touchline was almost full and there was still a good 40 minutes before the teams were due to appear. He'd never seen a crowd like it at any sporting fixture.

He looked down at his programme and smiled as he saw the prominent advertisement for the J.P. Surrey Driver cricket bat, as endorsed by his old friend C.B. Fry. Most of the names on the team sheet beneath were unfamiliar to him, although he knew of Billy Wedlock, the Bristol City half-back who was the pivot of the team.

'Your lads are missing a couple of good men today, Doctor,' said the man in the seat in front, twisting to address him, 'I don't fancy their chances much, I'm afraid.'

'Is that right?' he responded. 'I must confess not to being as knowledgeable as I should be.'

'Yes, Rippon and Marr, both injured. The other bad news for the Bristol lads is that Billy Meredith is playing.'

Ah yes, Meredith, he'd read about the players' union and its agitation for the abolition of football's maximum wage. He didn't see the problem: the cricket professionals often took on other employment during the winters if they weren't required to tour; why couldn't the footballers do the same in the summer?

A round of applause broke out around him and he saw Lord Charles Beresford being presented to the crowd on the open patch of turf between the grandstands and the pitch. Still widely appreciated for his activities in command of the fleet in Egypt and Sudan in the eighties and now in charge of the Channel Fleet, Beresford was a popular national figure and quite a coup as guest of honour for the Football Association. 'Rule,

Britannia!' rang out, then the national anthem, and when the ball boys were given a warm ovation as they ran to their positions around the field even an ostensibly disinterested spectator like Grace couldn't fail to be struck by the warmth of the atmosphere and the sense of excitement that thrummed through the entire stadium.

Bristol City appeared first, running on to the field in a change strip of blue shirts and long white shorts, leaping for imaginary headers and bouncing on the balls of their feet. Their support in a crowd that he estimated at somewhere in excess of 70,000 gave them a terrific reception, blue favours being waved in the air and rattles being lustily employed. Manchester United followed them on to the field in an all-white strip with a red V on the breast and the roar that greeted them, Grace felt, could conceivably have been heard in Manchester.

There was a pageantry about the occasion, he noted. Cricket, for all its rituals and traditions, didn't have the same sense of gladiatorial formality as this. Despite the party atmosphere and the noisy excitement of the crowd, the match itself was not a particularly memorable spectacle. Bristol City opened brightly – an early shot from inside-right Bob Hardy was well smothered by Moger in the United goal and caused the Doctor to scrunch his programme in his fist with excitement – but the incisive movement and passing of the forwards in white were giving the Bristol defence all kinds of problems. It was midway through the first half when Harold Halse hit a terrific shot that thudded on to the Bristol City crossbar, where it fell to Sandy Turnbull barely five yards out. Harry Clay in the City goal could only watch helplessly as the forward lashed the ball into the net.

There was an explosion of noise, so loud that it appeared to Grace to make the very air itself crackle and the Old Man was almost bewildered by it: it was like all the ovations he'd ever received replayed all at once. The white-shirted players ran to the prostrate Turnbull who'd only been a last-minute selection as he was carrying an injury, then trotted back to their own half for the game to restart.

Grace replayed the goal over and over in his mind, seeing the ball whack the crossbar and bounce down to the feet of Turnbull, who brought it under control apparently by sheer instinct and, almost in the same movement, thumped it into the net.

That must be the moment, he thought. For association footballers, that must be the equivalent of that suspension of time and age and occasion when the ball is on its way to the batsman. In the same way, Turnbull saw the ball coming to him off the crossbar and everything must have melted away to a cocoon of man and ball. Striking the ball would have provided the release and seeing it hit the net like seeing the ball skimming across the turf to the boundary.

Yet footballers played for only 90 minutes and had barely a handful of opportunities to experience the moment the way a cricketer does. For a great cricketer, there can be hundreds of those moments in a single match.

The rest of the game saw the northern side snuff out all of Bristol City's best efforts and, even though only one goal separated the teams, the result was never particularly in doubt. Grace was disappointed for his home-town team but as a sporting encounter he'd found the match unengaging. What had most caught his attention, however, was the nature of the crowd. It was enormous, and kept up a constant level of noise and excitement, rows and rows of flat caps with flashes of red and blue. Beer bottles piled up at the front of the enclosure opposite the pavilion, peanut sellers walked in front of them, tossing their wares to the customers with commendable accuracy. And the poor beggars had to go all the way back to Bristol and Manchester, arriving home at goodness knows what time, disgorged again from cold, draughty third-class compartments into the night air. But still they were happy and had many a tale to take back with them, especially the victorious Lancastrians.

He was suddenly gripped by a wave of glumness. This game, he thought, is the future. It's self-contained, over in two hours, it gives a quick fix of thrill and excitement, making it easier for the working man to fit into his weekly schedule: in following the flow of the football match he could work off all his frustrations and annoyances. The whole range of emotions of a three-day cricket match were compressed into two hours of association football. Starting matches at 3 p.m. on a Saturday suited the working hours and way of life of those employed in the factories, mills and pits. These teams represent smaller communities, towns and cities rather than whole counties, and the arenas are in the heartlands of the spectators themselves. The game has almost come to them, Grace thought, whereas cricket demands the people come to it.

The final whistle brought a roar from the crowd almost as loud as that which had greeted the goal, comprising a mixture of delight and relief. The teams shook hands as the supporters of both teams applauded, and trooped towards the presentation table that had been set up in front of the pavilion, right in front of Grace. Lord Beresford addressed the gathering. Nobody left: the crowd waited patiently to see Meredith awarded the cup.

Beresford's words did nothing to alleviate the Doctor's unease.

'The game of football is a national game that encourages the best characteristics of the British race,' he said. 'To play the game of football it is necessary for a man to be fit and in good health, and it was those characteristics that made the nation what it is today. The more the game is encouraged, the better.'

With that, he shook hands with Meredith and, to loud cheers, presented him with the trophy. W.G. hauled himself to his feet, excused himself as he made his way along the row expressing a desire to leave before the majority of the crowd began filling the streets. As he left the pavilion and walked briskly towards the park gates, he looked over towards the cricket ground. The London County experiment had failed. Despite a first-class cricket club appearing in their midst, the crowds had never come. They'd lost their first-class status in 1904 but had still turned out a pretty exceptional team for a couple of years after that. The Australians had come three times, the South Africans and the West Indians had also played on that field. The club had given opportunities to some excellent young players. But you can't force people to come and you can't impose allegiance. The silhouette of the pavilion loomed dark before a pink and purple sunset, its empty verandah looking out blindly across an empty field. There would be no fixtures this season and the club was in the process of being wound up. As he progressed through his cricketing twilight, was the game to which he'd devoted his life going to follow suit? He thrust his hands deep into the pockets of his overcoat, put his head down and walked home feeling old and tired.

Monday 21 May 1911

He asked Eva to prepare his funeral suit for the journey and turned to look out of the window. The newspaper was on the bed, its stark headline, 'DEATH OF DR E.M. GRACE', following him around the room. He'd barely slept for the last two nights since the news of Ted's death arrived late on Saturday evening. He'd been ill for some time – hearing how the previous summer he'd collapsed while batting for Thornbury at Weston and had to be carried from the field practically unconscious, never to play again, had troubled W.G. greatly – and his passing had been largely expected, but still, when the news came it caused the Old Man's legs to buckle and he had to reach out for the wall to stop himself falling.

Of all the Graces it was E.M. who'd seemed likeliest to go on for ever. Seven years his junior, W.G. had grown up in Ted's shadow until he was old enough first to match then eclipse his elder brother's cricketing prowess. However if E.M. had not spent so much time fulfilling his duties as the Coroner for the Lower Division of Gloucestershire then he may well have shown himself to be the better player. As it was he carried on playing for the county until he was 56 and scored, W.G. had estimated, something like 76,000 runs and taken somewhere north of 12,000 wickets.

Since the death of their parents Ted had been the one he knew he could turn to if necessary. They didn't have a warm relationship; it was more a deep mutual respect, but the baton denoting the head of the Grace family that had passed from their father to Ted now passed to him. He wasn't sure he wanted it. What he wanted was Ted back. Even though they rarely saw each other these days, he was reassured by his elder brother's presence in the world. He wanted Ted to be there, all mutton chop whiskers and irascibility, the Ted who once chased a spectator out of the ground and down the street for a cheeky remark, or bowled out batsmen with steepling lobs that landed on top of the stumps, causing the crowd and the opposition to react with such opprobrium that he had to pull up a stump in self-defence. That was Ted, not the man reduced to a bedridden husk of recent times.

He thought back to their childhood games at Downend, the endless summer evenings with the Graces at play, E.M. and Uncle Pocock leading the way, teasing the youngsters, giving them interminable sessions in the field while they dominated the batting and the bowling. Even back then the youthful W.G. could only watch his brother in awe. His timing with the bat was always exquisite: it didn't matter whether the ball was a good length, overpitched or a long-hop,

E.M. always seemed to meet it with the middle of the bat and send it to wherever he pleased. When he was a boy, Mr Cave's wood and quarry at long-on seemed to be popular destinations for the ball whenever Ted had the bat in his hand. The young W.G. would frequently emerge from the wilds covered in sap or quarry dust, occasionally both.

E.M. had also pioneered the art of hitting across the line. And in Grace's view it was indeed an art. In the boys' early days in the game scoring runs to leg was frowned upon as vulgar, even ungentlemanly. Ted paid no heed – possibly, W.G. thought, because as a small boy Ted had been coached using a full-sized bat and hence couldn't help but play across the line – and developed a vicious pull shot that was now in common use and praised to the heavens when executed properly.

E.M. was a breathtaking cricketer. Never had the Old Man seen someone who could take a match by the scruff of the neck and dominate it the way his brother did. He'd once heard it remarked that the only thing Ted couldn't do on a cricket field was keep wicket off his own bowling. Playing for Berkeley against Knole Park in 1861, he recalled, of a total of 119 Ted made 100 not out, then took all ten Knole Park wickets in the second innings. The same month he scored an unbeaten 119 for Lansdown and then bowled out the entire Clifton side. People still talked about the occasion the following year when he hit an undefeated 192 for MCC and took ten

Kent wickets in their second innings. He was the most complete cricketer the Old Man had ever seen and had been right from a young age: at 13 he was playing for West Gloucestershire against the famous All-England XI and more than holding his own.

The Champion had always felt that E.M. truly showed his character as a fielder. Ted would stand closer in at point than even he would dare, arguing that if the ball leapt off the pitch and took the bat high on the face or shoulder, he'd be in the perfect place to take the catch. He did, and frequently, but not all his catches were from plunging forward to scoop the ball into his hands as it dropped in front of the batsman. He once saw him catch a full-blooded drive from Stoddart barely six feet from the bat and calmly hand the ball to the wicketkeeper without so much as moving his feet. He also remembered Billy Murdoch middling a cut for the Australians in 1882 that E.M. pouched comfortably. Murdoch looked at him in disbelief and said, 'I thought it must have gone right through you.'

Grace also recalled the day in 1884 at Manchester when Gloucestershire were playing Lancashire. Their mother had been ill but not seriously enough to prevent the brothers going up to Manchester. The match had been interrupted by thunderstorms but Ted and W.G. went out to open the second innings with the scores relatively close and a telegram received that morning stating that their mother's condition was improving.

Characteristically, Ted drove the first ball of the innings for four runs. Twelve minutes before lunch, however, he was caught out at mid-off. W.G. walked to the wicket and had got off the mark and survived an appeal for leg before when Ted suddenly ran on to the field waving a telegram. Their mother, their dear, kind, devoted mother, had, it seemed, taken a major turn for the worse and died that morning. The two brothers stood on the field and looked at each other, frozen in shock and grief. Each searched the other's eyes, imploring them to do or say something, either to demonstrate the news wasn't true or to tell the other exactly what they should do next. The two greatest cricketers in the land were suddenly reduced to shocked, timid little boys. It took the Lancashire captain, their old friend 'Monkey' Hornby, to stride over, take both of them by the arm and announce the game was suspended and they should leave immediately for Bristol. Dear old Monkey, he walked them both from the field, into the pavilion and right to the changing room before telling them not to worry about a thing and that his sympathies, those of his team, his club and indeed of the whole cricket world were with them.

'What a terrible week, Eva,' he said, without turning away from the window. 'First Billy, now Ted.'

Ted had died just two days after the funeral of his close friend Billy Murdoch at Kensal Green. The Old Man had been unable to attend given he was waiting for news of E.M. and would have to leave for Thornbury at any moment. He'd felt agonised, for Murdoch had been probably his best friend in the game. They'd locked horns as adversaries on the field when he captained Australia but had also been regular team-mates, first for the Gentlemen and then for London County, when their deep friendship had been properly cemented. What a fine player he was, possibly the finest he'd ever seen aside from Ted. His cutting could make the Champion purr and his driving was immaculate. His 211 for Australia in 1884 at The Oval would always remain one of the finest innings Grace had ever witnessed by a player on an opposing team.

When Murdoch settled in England in 1890 to play for Sussex he and Grace became great friends. They liked to go shooting, they liked to play billiards late into the night and, when Grace had taken up golf in his later years, Murdoch was an enthusiastic protégé. W.G. saw something of himself in Billy – they shared the same determination to wring as much out of life as they possibly could and shared the same sense of fun and mischief. Billy had more stamina than most of Grace's friends and acquaintances and he also shared that innate competitiveness that drove him to keep playing and keep winning. Grace remembered with a smile an early game of golf in which Billy had found himself deep in a bunker. After a short while the ball appeared, bouncing on to the green after emerging over the lip of the bunker with a puff of sand. There were murmurs of appreciation from all those watching and it was only later, in the clubhouse, that Billy confessed quietly to him that he had picked up the ball with a handful of sand and lobbed it out of the bunker. Grace had roared with laughter.

He'd missed Billy Murdoch a great deal. A postcard from him the previous year confirmed that he and his wife would be coming back to England once they had sorted out the legal affairs of her late father, for which they had travelled back to Australia early in 1910. He remembered how Billy had laughed as he'd told Grace that his father-in-law couldn't stand him. He'd met Minnie on the long voyage back to Australia after the 1884 tour. Murdoch was still buoyant after his double-century at The Oval and when he'd seen Minnie on the deck, travelling back to Australia after completing her education in Europe, he was instantly smitten. Her father, who had made a considerable fortune from gold mining, certainly didn't want a cricketer for a son-in-law and made it clear to Minnie the relationship could not continue. Despite this they were married in Melbourne before the year was out and the Old Man knew they would have been smitten to the end.

He turned away from the window and went downstairs to his study. Pulling open a drawer in his desk and lifting some papers, he took out the postcard, the last direct communication he'd had with Billy Murdoch, and read it over and over again.

'See you next year for golf and guns, Gilbert!' were the closing words. If only. Poor Minnie had been at his side when he'd died back in February. It was so sudden and cruel. Billy had been watching the Test match between Australia and South Africa at the Melbourne Cricket Ground. From what the Old Man had heard, he'd taken lunch in the pavilion with the Melbourne Cricket Club committee and was talking to Major Morkham when he suddenly winced and put his hand to his head. The major asked what was wrong, he'd shaken his head and said, 'Neuralgia', then collapsed on to the floor.

Several doctors were close at hand, one of whom made an incision in Billy's wrist in an attempt to ease the pressure of blood on his brain before he was taken to a local private hospital. He never regained consciousness and died at five o'clock that afternoon with Minnie distraught at his bedside.

Grace had learned later the couple had been due to sail for England the following week.

Billy left instructions that he wanted to be buried near his mother at Kensal Green Cemetery in north London: his body, that proud, sturdy, vigorous physique, had been embalmed and transported back to England. It was an appropriate journey in many ways as that sea passage between the two nations had come to define his life and achievements.

Grace dropped the postcard on to the desk and sat looking at his hands, fingers linked, in his lap. It was so

much to take in. Not only had he lost a brother and a
friend, two enormous personalities had been snuffed
out and cricket, nay, the world were poorer places for
the absence of both.

He stroked his beard, stood up, walked to the back
door of the house, put on the boots that he always kept
there and strode into the garden to check on his
asparagus beds. With Billy's funeral occurring so long
after his death it was almost as if he were being mourned
twice. And Ted, explosive, opinionated Ted, what a force
has been snuffed out there. Two heavy emotional blows,
two thumping reminders of his own mortality, and in
the space of barely two days. He moved from the beds to
the putting green he'd carefully tended since they'd
moved to the house in Mottingham Lane. He toed away
a couple of leaves and trod down the grass around the
hole, wishing hard that he could look up and see Billy
striding towards him, putter over his shoulder, one hand
in his trouser pocket, moustache twitching and calling
out, 'Ho, Gilbert, where do you keep your golf balls?'

He was dreading E.M.'s funeral. At each of these
occasions the number of Graces of his era was declining
significantly, but Ted's would be particularly hard. Now
only young Alfred and himself remained of the five
Grace boys. Fred's death had been the hardest, being so
sudden and so desperately unfair given his youth. Henry
had been 63 when he died after suffering a stroke while
out shooting in Devon in 1895. W.G. wondered whether

anyone had got word of Ted's death to their cousin Walter Gilbert, in family-imposed Canadian exile after the scandal of being caught red-handed stealing money from the clothes of his East Gloucestershire team-mates in the dressing-room back in '86. So close had they been as youths Walter had been effectively an extra Grace brother.

And, of course, there were Bertie and Bessie, his own children, whom he and Agnes had had to bury. It seemed as if death was all around him these days.

Friday 20 February 1914

He left the warmth of the Oddfellows Hall and felt the chill air on his face, sucking the cold air deep into his lungs. Outside the cricket season these were his favourite kinds of morning: a low, golden sun casting warming light over the bare branches of the trees and dispelling a faint dusting of frost, a good breakfast inside him and the mass high-pitched yelping of the beagles.

'It's a fine day for it, Doctor,' said his friend Charles Blundell, with whom he'd stayed the previous night at his farmhouse a few miles away.

'The best, Blundell, the very best. And no finer outfit than the Halstead Place Beaglers to spend it with.'

The leader of the hunt emerged from the hall in green jacket and cap, white breeches, and boots.

'A fine pack today, Mr Russell,' said Grace. 'How many couples?'

'Seventeen and a half, Doctor. Always have a good pack at Edenbridge.'

'I'm looking forward to this morning very much, Mr Russell. I've not been out with the hounds nearly as much as I'd like this winter.'

'I wish you an excellent day, Dr Grace.'

He surveyed the scene, the animation of the dogs' raised tails, the bright green of the hunt officials' jackets, the knots of people talking excitedly, the clouds of breath, the thumped greetings of gloved hands on shoulders, and felt very much alive. He would be 66 this summer and still intended to play as often as he could for Eltham. Though he was hardly an asset in the field any more, even in the reduced circumstances of local club cricket, his eye was keen enough and he could still destroy a good-standard club bowling attack with ruthless efficiency. Walking after the hounds today was a perfect aid to rebuilding his stamina for the coming season. He anticipated a good six hours of hunting today and the thought of it stirred up the flutter of anticipation. It was always around this time of year, when the dark curtains of the day's extremities began to draw back and the weather began to improve, that the old stomach butterflies about the coming season really began to find their rhythm. He was thankful that the enthusiasm never dimmed, that the end of winter and the first signs of impending spring brought such a keen sense of anticipation now, in 1914, just as it had as far back as 1860.

His appetite for following the hounds hadn't dimmed either in as many years, from the moment he'd first heard the yelp of the Clifton Beagles bounding through the trees behind Downend as a boy. Since moving to south London he'd joined the Worcester Park Beagles but couldn't get out with them as much as he liked any more. Fortunately his old friend Blundell always had a bed for him whenever he wanted to come down and see the Halstead Place team and he took up the offer whenever his schedule allowed.

Blundell appeared at his shoulder, pulled out a hip flask and offered Grace a nip.

'No thanks, old friend, I'm warm enough with the anticipation, that's plenty for me.'

'One never grows tired of it, does one? The hounds, I mean.'

'It would be no kind of life any more if one did. No kind of life at all. Imagine a life without the "tallyho" coming across the fields.'

Three short notes sounded on a huntsman's bugle. The hounds were prepared and ready.

'We shall hear it shortly, I feel,' said Blundell, and with that the hounds were released and a tan, black and white melee bundled past them and out into the field.

'Follow me, Charles, and good hunting.'

The Old Man took long, heavy strides into the tall grass, his stick whirling in his right hand, his long shadow stretching behind him as he walked towards the rising sun.

Tuesday 23 June 1914

The Grand Hall of the Hotel Cecil certainly lived up to its name: a high, vaulted ceiling and gilt-dripped ornamentation rose like a cathedral over the long tables. At first he thought it was odd not to have the Lord's centenary dinner anywhere near Lord's, but he had to admit, for an event on this scale and of this importance, the decision to hold it here had been a good one. Plus it was almost next door to Charing Cross station, meaning he could be home in no time once the speeches and toasts were completed.

It was also – he'd been through his records to check – almost exactly 50 years since his own first appearance at Lord's, four days after his 16th birthday for South Wales against MCC. It was just after he'd made 170 for the same side against the Gentlemen of Sussex at Hove. He had fond memories of that match, for it was the first time he'd played with an entire absence of nerves. He no longer felt like a boy among men: when he began playing his shots he realised that he had the measure of the bowlers and there was no reason at all to be apprehensive. Since that day, a month shy of half a century ago, he couldn't remember ever being nervous on a cricket field. He'd become curiously dry-mouthed as he worked his way through the nineties during his 100th century but he just put that down to the significance of the occasion; it certainly hadn't been what he'd call nerves.

Yes, that innings at Hove changed things for ever, he recalled. It meant that the game against MCC at Lord's a week later had held no fear at all for him. He'd heard bad things about the wicket, though, and when he walked out to bat at the fall of the second wicket on the first day he saw that the horror stories had been right. The creases were actually dug out of the turf, inch-wide trenches burrowing across the square, which was also scattered with pieces of gravel. It wasn't until poor George Summers was killed in 1870 that any serious thought was given to the state of the Lord's wicket.

It was a challenge for a lad of tender years but he just thought about each ball as it came, playing it off the pitch as much as he could, and helped to get the South Walians out of a scrape at 17 for three by scoring exactly 50 before being bowled by a shooter from Arthur Teape. His was the second highest score of the innings.

It was astounding to think that had been 50 years ago. To think he was here, celebrating its centenary, when he'd first played at Lord's half the ground's lifetime ago.

The occasion was slightly more subdued than expected after the news earlier in the week that A.G. Steel had died suddenly at the age of 55. He'd made the first Test match hundred at Lord's, an immaculate 148 against Australia in 1884, and was as good a slow bowler as he was a batsman.

Lord Hawke presided as President of MCC with the late Queen's grandson Prince Albert of Schleswig-Holstein, a bowler of surprisingly good leg-breaks, seated to his right. As part of his toast Hawke looked back over the previous century at Lord's and predicted that the ground, MCC and the game of cricket itself would still be flourishing a century hence.

'The fact that there are sixteen first-class counties where once there were only eight, besides twenty minor counties, shows that cricket is progressing and still has its fair share of public support,' he said. 'In recent times there has been much criticism and talk of slow cricket, which is all very well but the science of placing the field and accurate bowling surely has something to do with it.

'We are fortunate this evening to be honoured by the presence of the great Dr W.G. Grace,' he continued, but before he could complete his sentence applause washed forward from the back of the room and everyone was on their feet except the Champion himself. He raised himself briefly from his seat in acknowledgment and sat down again.

'There have been such cricket geniuses in the past,' continued Hawke, 'and so there will continue to be in the future. We might not have such idols as W.G. Grace, Ranji, Stoddart, Jackson, Jessop and Hirst in their prime, but I believe they will come tomorrow as they have come before.'

It needled the Old Man slightly that he was being referred to as part of the past – after all, was he not still making runs for Eltham? – but he was aware that no slight was meant by it and he didn't take it as one. At length it was his turn to respond to the toast. He rose slowly from his seat and looked out at the sea of faces. The now customary ovation eventually died away.

'I thank you, gentlemen, for the great reception you have afforded me here this evening. There has been much talk of the past and the future from my friend and colleague Lord Hawke, but may I remind the company that cricket was just as good in the old days it is now.

'I am an old man now, and if I may make one observation about the modern game it is that young players today do not make sufficient use of their legs.'

There was much laughter at this and the Champion was briefly flustered.

'I should hasten to explain,' he continued, 'that I mean the use of the legs in batting, by such players as Sir T.C. O'Brien, running out to slow bowlers and hitting them for four and the like.'

Cheers and applause greeted this analysis.

'I shall not crave your indulgence any longer, and instead defer in favour of those more qualified to speak on such an auspicious occasion as this than I am.'

There was another long ovation and it was several minutes before the MP Walter Long could propose a toast to 'imperial cricket', adding, 'the game has strength-ened the bonds of Empire, and, in the expressions "that is cricket" and "it is not cricket" the game has provided phrases defining the highest standard of honour'.

Half an hour later Grace walked out of the hotel and turned left towards the station. He had a few minutes before his train so he walked down the hill and crossed the street to the bank of the Thames. A few steam barges sailed back and forth, black silhouettes against the light reflecting from the surface of the water.

He'd felt old tonight. He *was* old, there was no escaping that, but he didn't often feel it the way he had this evening. Many of the young men in the room, their eyes flashing with youthful happiness and wine in the soft light of the candelabras, would never have seen him play in his most prolific years. Some wouldn't even have been born.

Yet for all the talk of the future and the boisterous joy that infused the atmosphere in the room, he couldn't quite share the naked optimism with which the air positively thrummed. When he looked around the candle-lit faces at some of the young players he recognised, he felt almost like an old schoolmaster, chalking off another generation to add to all those that had gone before. Yet there was something about the occasion that nagged at him. Maybe it was because it came so hard on the heels of Allan Steel's death: he should have been there, should have shared the occasion, adding his own anecdotes to the post-prandial reminiscence with brandy in hand. He couldn't quite put his finger on it but something seemed to be tugging at the fringes of his soul, something elusive but something that came with a sense of foreboding.

It was probably just the fact that the world was changing, and changing so fast. Lord's itself was practically unrecognisable from the semi-rural cabbage patch on to which he'd walked for the first time that hot July day in 1864. There had been no grandstand and no nursery, while the tavern was a ramshackle affair far removed from the current incarnation. The Pavilion was now nearly 25 years old and he was the only one still calling it the 'new' pavilion.

For most of the summer he'd had to bat with a runner as he'd become so slow between the wickets. He rarely bowled, and if he did it was only a couple of overs at a time. His old team-mates and colleagues were all dying off: the visitors arriving at Fairmount to play billiards and whist and talk about the old days were becoming fewer and fewer. Maybe that was why this sense of portent was tugging at him, just out of view.

Yes, that must be it, he thought. I'm just an old man. I'm young in my mind and young in my heart, and as my batting averages prove I'm young in my eye. Everything else is old and decaying. That, he thought, must be the only thing to account for the sense of ennui he'd felt at the dinner this evening and lay behind a vague sense, just a shimmer at the edges of his being, of impending doom.

A steam tug emerged from under the bridge and sounded its whistle. A train pulled out of the station above, chuffing white smoke into the night sky. The old man turned away from the dark water and made his way back up the hill to the station.

Thursday 16 July 1914

He showed the man from the *Morning Post* into his office, invited him to take a seat and sat down at his desk. He rarely gave interviews, especially these days, but when the *Post* had approached him about marking his 66th birthday with a large feature he agreed readily, for he had a few opinions to share.

Eva brought in the tea tray, Grace asked after the man's journey, he replied that it was fine but a longer walk from the station than he had anticipated, the tea was poured, they exchanged shared agreement about the growing seriousness of the international situation, the man pulled his notebook from his attaché case and they began.

'I'll commence with a big question if I may, Doctor,' he said. 'Are the cricketers of today better than those of the past? For example, modern critics often tell us that such bowlers as Barnes are better than any of their predecessors, and that footwork has revolutionised the art of modern batting.'

Grace thought for a moment and then leaned forward in his chair.

'It would more sensible,' he said, 'to say "one of the best" instead of "the best" when the leading bowlers and batsmen of today are praised. After all, these critics do not remember the old days; why, they were not even born then. There are many more first-rate cricketers today than there were two generations or even a single generation ago. Naturally so; for much more cricket is played and there are so many more playing now, that the number of those who play well is necessarily larger than it used to be. But the best men of the past were easily as good, I should say, as the best men of the present.

'Footwork is certainly not a new discovery,' he continued. 'The idea of teaching young batsmen not to move their right foot at the crease was to prevent them from drawing away towards short leg, which is in my opinion the worst of all batting faults and the worst of all weak batting habits. It means first of all that the bat is not held straight' – he was out of his seat now, and had picked up a poker from the fire grate that he was employing as a bat – 'and, secondly, that the batsman does not get over the ball, which is the secret of all successful batting.'

He was lunging forward now, playing a defensive shot with the poker, making the tea tray rattle, his head over where he imagined the ball to be. He held the shot steady, perfectly balanced. Even on the eve of his 66th birthday, even on the slippery rug in his office, everything was in the right place just as it had been under the watchful eye of Uncle Pocock and his mother back at Downend 60 years earlier.

He straightened, took a step backwards and sat down again, still holding the poker.

'I believe firmly in good footwork and always have done, but pulling away from wicket and footwork are very different matters, very different indeed, and should not be confused. Footwork comes with experience, after a batsman has learned to take up a proper position at the crease and has the confidence to attack the ball.'

He was up out of his seat again and it struck the man from the *Morning Post* how light he was on his feet for a man of his age and size. The Champion swished up the poker in a perfect backlift, took a large step forward with his left foot, drew up his right, stepped forward again and swished the poker as if he were launching an errant lob high into the Lord's Pavilion. The journalist felt the breeze as the poker passed a little closer to his ear than ideally he would have liked.

'I do not for an instant suggest that a batsman should run out to every slow ball bowled to him,' said Grace, warming further to his theme and pointing the poker at his visitor as he took his seat again, 'but when a ball is bowled high in the air it is certainly a very good policy to go out and make it full pitch.'

The journalist drew breath to ask another question but his subject was not yet done with the first.

'Again,' he said, 'in comparing the old players and those of today you must remember that the former did not have the same advantages as those playing today.

The pitches were not nearly as good. I was only thinking the other day about how Lord's was very bad at times during my younger days. There were no boundaries meaning every hit had to be run out, making the work of reaching a big score much harder then than it is now. Games were stopped for rain, but it was not customary in the old days to wait for the ground to dry, we just went out again as soon as the rain stopped even when the bowlers and fieldsmen could hardly keep their footing.

'The game was never stopped for bad light, either, although there is some excuse for that innovation at Lord's, for example, where the light is not as good as it was before the Mound Stand and the present Pavilion were built. Indeed, the same may be said of other grounds.'

He paused for a moment and gazed out of the window. The journalist tried to seize the moment, but again barely had a chance to draw breath before his interviewee was off again.

'It does seem to me that there is not as much fun in first-class cricket as there used to be,' he lamented. 'County cricket is taken far too seriously these days. There is too much of it and it has become too much of a business. I think it would be a better competition if more amateurs were included in the county elevens. The man who can only play occasionally ought to have a chance of playing if he is really good.

'There are too many first-class counties, too, I think, and it's clear that some of these will not be able to stand the expense much longer. Personally I should like to see Gloucestershire and Somerset combine forces with half the home matches being played in each county. They would then have one strong side instead of two weak ones.'

And so the afternoon continued. The journalist gave up his planned interrogation and simply listened and scribbled silently while the Champion held forth with a torrent of opinion and suggestions on the improvement of the modern game, occasionally leaping up from his chair and playing more shots with the poker.

Two hours had passed before the man was able to extricate himself from his verbal machine-gunning. He would walk back to Eltham and Mottingham station, catch the train, begin rifling through the pages of notes he'd transcribed trying to work out how he was going to reduce it all to 1,200 words by deadline time, look out of the window at the terraced streets of south London whooshing by and realise that the conversation he'd just had was that of a man who'd not had such a conversation in a long time. He'd disembark at Charing Cross, make his way back to the office, dump his notes on to his desk and tell his colleagues about how this remarkable old cricketer had, on the eve of his 66th birthday, given him one of the most animated, detailed and fascinating interviews of his career.

When he sat down at his desk he recalled just how struck he'd been by the contrast between the tired, stooped, faintly ill-looking old man with whom he'd exchanged small talk about the prospects of war, and the giant, charismatic presence with sparkling eyes and the footsteps of a dancer, swishing a poker around a suburban study while his eyes shone and sparkled as he lost himself completely in the moment.

Saturday 25 July 1914

He was a week into his 67th year and feeling on top of the world as he walked from the wicket to the applause of the smattering of spectators around the boundary of the Grove Park ground on Marvels Lane, conveniently the closest pitch to his home aside from the pitches at the school for missionaries' sons that had taken over the old Royal Naval College across the road from Fairmount.

He'd gone in at the fall of the fourth wicket when there had been barely 20 runs on the board. The sun was warm on his back, his bat felt light in his hands and his legs thrummed with an energy rarely felt in recent years. It had turned out to be one of those days when everything just seemed to go right. His footwork was as nimble as it had been in 30 years and his timing of the ball took older spectators back to the glory days of full houses at The Oval. He drove with immense power, the bat coming down in a perfect arc, the middle of the bat meeting the ball and sending it skimming over the turf to the boundary.

With Eagleton first, then Henshall, he restored the Eltham score to a wholly respectable 155 for six when the declaration came at the tea interval. With his 69 not out the Champion had made nearly half the runs and he was beaming widely behind that vast grey beard as he walked back to the pavilion with an agility he could barely recognise.

It didn't matter that this was Marvels Lane, Grove Park, rather than Lord's. It didn't matter that the opposition was a clubbable bunch of clerks, solicitors and the son of the local vicar rather than 'the Demon' Spofforth or Charlie Kortright. It didn't matter that the game was watched by barely a hundred picnicking locals enjoying a hot Saturday afternoon in the sunshine for whom the cricket was incidental rather than a noisy capacity crowd at The Oval or the Melbourne Cricket Ground. As ever, once the ball left the bowler's hand absolutely nothing mattered other than his duel with it. The years fell away, the occasion melted to nothing and there was just him and the ball, locked in a duel that on this occasion he won convincingly.

How he lived for those moments, when he wasn't an aching, ageing, fading grey-bearded colossus whose body was not keeping up with the quickness of his mind and the vigour of his soul. What on earth would he ever do without them?

'Well played, Father,' he heard his son Charles saying as he reached the boundary, 'well played.'

'A shame you weren't still out there with me, Charles,' he replied, clapping his boy on the back with a giant, meaty hand.

'There'll be other occasions I'm sure. If I faced that ball a hundred more times I'd never nick it behind like that again,' said Charles with a faint shrug.

'There's always next week, my boy. Always next week.'

He clumped up the wooden steps, turned into the dressing-room, dropped his bat and gloves on to his battered old leather cricket bag and sat down to unbuckle his pads. The way he felt at that moment he could have batted on all day and come back tomorrow and batted some more. But, yes, there was always next week.

Eltham worked hard in the field, the Old Man appealing from point for decisions he had no right to with the same gusto as ever, and Charles took four for 48, but Grove Park held on gamely for an honourable draw, finishing the day on 99 for eight. It was a most familiar scene as the players trooped off applauding the two batsmen who'd resolutely blocked out the final overs. White-clad figures in the golden evening light, their shadows growing longer on the grass, the thrumming of an afternoon's exertions in their limbs, a church clock striking seven thirty, honours even, the cricketing gods satisfied, and among them a tall man in a white sunhat, a grey beard hanging down past his breastbone, shirt and trousers hanging more loosely than they once had, congratulating the batsmen and the bowlers, not least his own offspring, and thinking that this was about as perfect a day as he could remember for a long time.

W.G. Grace – the Champion, the Old Man, the Doctor, Gilbert – had just played the last innings of his life.

Tuesday 4 August 1914

'Owing to the summary rejection by the German Government of the request made by his Majesty's Government for assurances that the neutrality of Belgium will be respected, his Majesty's Ambassador to Berlin has received his passports, and his Majesty's Government declared to the German Government that a state of war exists between Great Britain and Germany as from 11 p.m. on August 4, 1914.'

Saturday 8 August 1914

As the afternoon moved wearily towards evening it became clear that he wouldn't be required to bat. He was a little disappointed – it was after all the only significant contribution he could make to the team these days – but there was also a rare hint of relief. His mind had been occupied this week by thoughts of war and death. The build-up to the conflict with Germany had remained largely on the periphery of his priorities in recent weeks other than a mild concern about his son Edgar, a commander in the Royal Navy and currently preparing his ship, HMS *New Zealand*, for impending conflict, but the actual declaration of war unsettled him. War wasn't something he understood particularly, not something that had ever impinged upon his life. The confident assertions of some that it would all be over by Christmas reassured him slightly but his world had been set askew on its axis. Normally his son Charles would have been here too but, now a qualified engineer, he had enlisted in the No. 4 Electric Light Company of the Kent Fortress Royal Engineers and had already motorcycled down to Sheerness where he was to oversee their coastal searchlights. Already it felt faintly wrong to be here, to be playing cricket in the sunshine while the nation prepared for war. Part of him thought that this scene, the cricketers on the field with the trees in the background, the men in straw boaters and the women with parasols strolling around the boundary, was in part what the country was fighting to preserve. But the fact there was fighting to be done – and that his sons would most probably be doing some of it – made this tranquil scene feel somehow inappropriate.

He didn't fully understand the political and military ins and outs that had led to the conflict but he knew this was an issue for the entire nation. The more he looked out across the field at the familiar rhythms, rituals and choreographies of the game, the more detached it seemed from the necessary international task at hand.

And then there was Trotty. Poor old Albert had shot himself the previous week in his lodgings at Harlesden. He wasn't a close friend but the Old Man had always enjoyed his company: he was a huge personality full of amusing stories, and Grace had always greatly admired him as a cricketer, too. He'd always be remembered for hitting the ball clean over the Lord's Pavilion, something nobody else had emulated. His memories of Trotty were all infused with laughter. To think of him, alone in a room, cradling a pistol in his hands preparing to end his life served only to reinforce the gloom in Grace's heart.

He sat alone on a bench in front of the pavilion watching the field change after the penultimate over. The umpires in their straw boaters and long white coats each took their measured steps between square leg and the wickets like two figures from a cuckoo clock. The white-clad fielders converged on the square and spread again, like a flower closing and opening towards the sun.

War never petered out like this. There was always a result and the entire nation needed to ensure that the outcome was the right one. It was that simple.

As the dead game went through the motions of its final over a cloud passed across the sun. The last ball was defended back to the bowler, the umpire called time and removed the bails, there was a pitter-patter of applause from the field and the ragged, sun-weary procession began to make its way towards the pavilion. There was a scraping of tin as someone began to remove the numbers from the scoreboard and drop them in an untidy pile.

The Old Man heaved himself up from his bench and took a few stiff steps across the boundary rope towards the gaggle of players. He shook hands with the batsmen, the umpires and every member of the opposing team and watched them go into the pavilion. He stood for a while, hands in trouser pockets, then began to walk out across the empty field, the bright green of the grass now showing a blueish sheen under the clouds. He reached the light strip of the pitch, naked without stumps at each end, the scratches and gouges from the day's play still visible. He walked to the crease at one end and placed his feet as he would if he were taking guard, held an imaginary bat and settled into his stance. He looked down at his feet placed either side of the crease and looked up the field, but saw neither an umpire leaning over the wicket with a sweater draped over his arm nor a bowler at the end of his run pushing his hair back from his forehead ready to commence his run-up; there was just an empty expanse of field with trees in the distance.

Tuesday 25 August 1914

Even an hour's putting practice couldn't quell the restlessness. He'd hoped the concentration and relaxation of a session on the green in the back garden at Fairmount would settle his mind but although he was sinking the ball nearly every time his mind remained curiously agitated. He was anxious about Edgar, 'the Commander' as he proudly called him, somewhere out on the North Sea with his ship. Charles was not in such immediate danger at Sheerness, and his regular visits – the sound of his motorcycle coming up the drive always gladdened his heart – reassured both him and Agnes on that front, but Grace remained perplexed by the war situation. For the first time in his life cricket wasn't the most important thing in the world. The war dominated his thoughts and he'd begun reading the newspaper reports closely every morning. The British Expeditionary Force was engaged at Mons and it sounded like a hell of a battle. It seemed as if they were holding their line and arresting the German sweep across Belgium into France, but he'd heard talk of more than two thousand British Expeditionary Force casualties already and couldn't bear it. All he could think of were Charles and the Commander, of how men just like them were falling in droves. He'd already buried two of his children; he couldn't countenance having to bury another.

And all the while cricket limped on. He'd been at Lord's a couple of weeks earlier for Hobbs's benefit. The Oval had been requisitioned as a stores depot so the match had been moved to St John's Wood and there was barely a crowd. Yet a week earlier, just before war was declared, 15,000 had turned out on the Bank Holiday Monday to see the same player score 226. The same day A.H. Hornby had been called away to the War Office as he was taking the field for Lancashire against Yorkshire at Old Trafford. While bowling at Trent Bridge, Nottinghamshire's Basil Melle had received a telegram summoning him to Oxford to join the University's regiment of the King's Colonial Corps.

He'd tried to balance the situation in his mind with the thought that cricket was doing its bit for morale, that it was good for the nation to keep some semblance of normal life and routine, but the empty grounds and the frightening reports of casualties from Mons had convinced him otherwise. Cricketers had no business playing on when men were dying in France.

In frustration he smacked a golf ball hard across the turf; the sound of it hitting the fence 30 yards away was like a rifle shot. He threw down the club and strode off back to the house.

He sat down hard in his chair, pulled himself towards the desk, picked up his pen and held it poised to write.

The page was blank but for the embossed 'Fairmount, Mottingham, Eltham, Kent' at the top. He wrote the date beneath it and began.

'Sir,' he wrote, paused for a moment, and then allowed the pen to scratch away uninterrupted.

There are many cricketers who are already doing their duty, but there are many more who do not seem to realise that in all probability they will have to serve either at home or abroad before the war is brought to a conclusion. The fighting on the Continent is very severe and will probably be prolonged. I think the time has arrived when the county cricket season should be closed, for it is not fitting at a time like this that able-bodied men should be playing day after day, and pleasure-seekers look on. There are so many who are young and able, and are still hanging back. I should like to see all first-class cricketers of a suitable age set a good example, and come to the aid of their country without delay in its hour of need.

Yours, etc.
W.G. Grace

He laid down the pen, picked up the letter and read it. Then he read it again, folded it, pushed it inside an envelope and sealed it.

He rummaged in a pile of papers until he found a copy of *The Sportsman* and leafed through its pages until he found the address he was after.

'The Editor, The Sportsman, Boy Court, Ludgate Hill, London EC,' he wrote, underlining with a flourish. He called for Eva, handed her the envelope and asked her to take it to the post office immediately.

Within days the County Championship was called off and Surrey declared champions. Even the traditional end-of-season Scarborough Festival was cancelled. The Old Man would not take all the credit but he allowed himself a degree of satisfaction to think that his contribution had been of some assistance. A few days later he was pleased to be able to add his name to an appeal on behalf of the Prince of Wales Fund that appeared in the newspapers across the land. On breakfast tables and omnibuses, in libraries and smoking rooms, the following message was read and digested:

TO THE CRICKET LOVING PUBLIC. Dear Sir. We, the undersigned, as cricketers, ask you to accord us the publicity which only your columns can give, in order that we may make a direct appeal to the vast cricket-loving public on behalf of the Prince of Wales Fund. This Fund, which has been called into being by His Royal Highness to meet the countless cases of misery and hardship which must inevitably follow on the heels of War, makes an instinctive and instantaneous appeal to the generosity of the public, and we as cricketers know that there is no public so sportsmanlike and so generous as the cricketing crowd.

As the Prince has truly said, 'this is a time when we all stand by one another'. All of us as a nation are members of a national team. We have before us as we write the vision of many a fair English cricket ground packed with eager multitudes. We have pleasant memories of the seas of faces which, in happier times, have watched us play. If only at this moment of trial we could gather in the sums which have been paid as gate-money at cricket matches, those on whom the war has laid a desolating hand would benefit indeed. The wives and families of our soldiers and sailors would, at least, be secure from want. It is this thought which has given rise to this particular appeal.

We ask those who have watched us play and who have cheerfully paid their half-crowns, shillings and sixpences as gate-money to step forward and contribute over again their half-crowns, shillings and sixpences to the Prince's Fund, out of gratitude for the enjoyment the cricket field has given them in the past.

Let everyone who has followed cricket call to mind the matches he has witnessed and enjoyed, and let each one contribute according to the pleasantness of their memories. Then we shall have for those whom the war has robbed not only of happiness, but even the means of livelihood, a truly royal sum.

Without any undue spirit of self-importance, we may perhaps say that we have contributed not a little to the interest the public takes in cricket, and, therefore, we make this personal appeal from ourselves to all those who love the game to send whatever they can spare to HRH. the Prince of Wales; Buckingham Palace, London, SW.

Yours faithfully,
J.W.H.T. Douglas, F.R. Foster,
F.H. Gillingham, W.G. Grace,
Harris, T. Hayward, G. Hirst,
J.B. Hobbs, G.L. Jessop, W. Rhodes,
R.H. Spooner, P.F. Warner, F.E. Woolley

Monday 23 May 1915

When he awoke that morning he knew there was no question of him playing. He hadn't picked up a bat in anger in more than a year. He'd barely bowled even in jest and he couldn't remember the last time he'd been out with the beagles.

He'd been torn when Alec Hearne's letter had arrived asking him to play. It was for a good cause – the Lewisham Red Cross Fund – and Catford was local enough for it not to be an inconvenience. It was Archie MacLaren's brainchild – he was stationed at Lewisham – and he'd be playing along with Jack Hobbs and 'Shrimp' Leveson Gower so there was a good prospect of a crowd. If W.G.'s name could be added to the poster the attendance was sure to buck up further.

Archie had come to visit the previous month with Ranji – both of them in uniform – and they'd enjoyed a splendid day reminiscing, putting, playing billiards and rounding off proceedings with a few hands of whist. Archie had sold the game to him in terms that genuinely made him think he could and would play.

It was at the end of the evening that the conversation turned more maudlin as they talked about poor Stoddart, another old colleague who'd died at his own hand the previous week.

'I hear that on the evening he died Andy was in a tremendous funk, picked up his pistol and announced he was tired of it all and going to finish it,' said MacLaren. 'Ethel pleaded with him not to and even struggled with him for possession of the gun, but when she noticed it wasn't loaded she relaxed a little, especially when she insisted he give her the box of cartridges which she went and locked away.

'He went upstairs and a short while later there was a loud bang. Ethel found him lying dead across the bed with a gunshot wound to his temple. The pistol was in his hand and there was a second box of cartridges on the bed, with one missing.'

The three of them were quiet for a moment, the old man with the long grey beard and tired eyes and the two khaki-clad officers, three of the greatest cricketers who had ever lived, staring silently into the flames of the fire and remembering a fourth. The Old Man thought of Ethel Stoddart, the feisty Australian singer who'd left her husband and travelled halfway round the world for Andy. Grace had travelled barely a mile to meet Agnes and certainly couldn't countenance ever leaving her in such a situation. The poor man had clearly taken leave of his senses.

'Poor Stoddy,' said W.G., eventually breaking the silence. The others murmured their agreement.

'Money worries, on top of everything else,' added MacLaren. 'Is money really worth taking your life for?'

'I imagine the lack of it possibly is,' said Ranji, and the trio lapsed into silence again.

'So many good ones gone, and before their time,' said the Old Man. 'So many.'

'Thank goodness you're still in rude health, Doctor,' said MacLaren.

'I wouldn't say that, Archie. I'm an old man now.'

He paused and looked into the fire again.

'Before long there will be no one left to call me Gilbert.'

He'd woken the next morning and immediately regretted agreeing to play. He lay in the dark looking at the stripe of sunlight arrowing across the ceiling through a small gap in the curtains. Ordinarily he'd have been looking forward to the game, but in the seven months since the beginning of the war he'd lost all his appetite for games. He traced it back to that last appearance for Eltham against Northbrook the previous summer, his first game since war had been declared. The desire for the moment had deserted him entirely. Not only that, he'd been having doubts about his earlier determination that cricketers should go off to fight. The casualty figures were growing every day and he couldn't help but think about how some of them may have been prompted to enlist by his letter to *The Sportsman*.

He was sick with worry about Edgar, now promoted from Commander to Captain, and when he'd read of the Battle of Heligoland knowing that he was out there in that cold, unforgiving North Sea he'd not slept for days until he heard for certain that the boy was all right. Charles still visited regularly from Sheerness and he was relieved his youngest son wasn't out in France or Belgium. He was maybe being oversensitive, but having buried Bertie and dear, dear Bessie already he didn't want to go through the same agony again, and he certainly didn't want Agnes to go through it too.

Agnes, he thought, had never got over Bessie. She was a wonderful woman still but he could sense that shadow in her soul because it matched his. If anything happened to Edgar or Charles he didn't think she'd survive it. And now he thought of all the mothers across the land collapsing to the floor with a scrunched telegram in their hands.

He couldn't play. That was clear. At the same time he'd given his word and his name would be on the posters. People would come to see him and the coffers would benefit. He'd have to come up with something.

When he arrived at the Catford ground the early arrivals were delighted to see him and there were shouts of greeting to which he raised his hat, a fair few handshakes and a 'I saw every run of your 152 against the Aussies at The Oval, Dr Grace' from a white-haired old gentleman.

MacLaren heard the commotion of his arrival and came out of the pavilion to greet him. His smile faded a little when he saw the Old Man.

'Where's your bag, Doctor?' he asked.

'Archie, I'm very sorry but I've been a little under the weather for the past two days,' he said. 'I'm afraid I'm not well enough to play and certainly not to justify keeping a younger, fitter man out of the team. I wouldn't miss the day for the world, though, so I thought I'd come here in person to tell you and stay for the match if that's amenable to you.'

'Amenable? Of course it's amenable, as long as your health allows it. It's wonderful to see you. I am very sorry that we won't have you on the field, but just having you here is reward enough. I can't thank you enough, Doctor.'

He took a seat in the front of the pavilion and picked up a collecting box, a wooden affair with a handle, whitewashed with a painted red cross.

He looked up and saw a man bending down and talking into the ear of the small red-haired boy in front of him, his son, about eight years old, pointing at the Old Man with one hand and pressing a sixpence into his palm with the other.

The boy walked nervously towards him. Grace opened up a beaming smile, put his hand out towards him and said, 'Come on, my boy, don't be shy.' The boy edged forward, his eyes on Grace, his mouth slightly open, held out the sixpence and dropped it into the collecting box with a wooden clunk. Grace reached out and ruffled his hair.

'Thank you, my boy, I hope you're the first of many today.'

MacLaren went out to toss and elected to bat. His was the stronger team and the crowd looked forward to seeing Hobbs. The disappointment of the Old Man's absence from the side would be tempered by the presence of the country's greatest current batsman.

The umpires walked out to the middle followed by the Catford team. MacLaren and David Mustard strode out to open the innings and a steady stream of well-wishers approached the Old Man to drop coins into his collecting box.

During a lull he closed his eyes in the sunshine and was aware of a shadow falling over him. He opened his eyes.

'Hello, Jack.'

'Hello, Doctor, good to see you.'

'I was very sorry about your benefit. A week earlier when you were making hay in the sunshine at The Oval …'

'Well, more important events intervened. It was good of you to come, though, I was very glad to see you.'

'Least I could do, Jack. You're the finest batsman in the game. I only hope this blasted war is over soon and doesn't disrupt your career for too long.'

'That's kind of you to say so.'

'Not opening today?'

'I'm going in at five.'

There was a round of applause for the fifty partnership.

'I hope we get to see you, these two look well set.'

'I hope so too. I always raise my game when you're in the ground, Doctor.'

'Are you playing much?'

'I'm going to be playing on Saturdays for Idle in the Bradford League. It's a good standard.'

'The leagues are still going even in the war?'

'The Bradford League, yes. I'm working in a munitions factory and doing some coaching at Westminster School during the week, but my Saturdays are free so I'm glad to play some good-standard cricket to keep my eye in until this mess is all over.'

'Good luck to you, Jack.'

Eventually Hobbs went out to bat. Of all the batsmen Grace had ever seen, he enjoyed watching Hobbs the most. His poise, his timing, his range of shots – he was the most complete batsman he'd ever seen and when war broke out he was just reaching his peak. He was a good name for Archie to secure with so many well-known cricketers away at the front.

When Hobbs had played himself in and looked well set, the Old Man got up and began to walk around the boundary with his collection box. Hobbs cut and drove and pulled with beautiful timing and made 126, 96 of them in boundaries and mostly in a partnership of 167 with Leveson Gower. Grace stopped and chatted with members of the crowd and held out his Red Cross box and at the end of the day was responsible for a sizable part of the £100 raised by the game.

The match ended in a draw and everyone was satisfied. He sat with the players for a while afterwards but didn't stay long as he was expecting a cable at home from Edgar. He said goodbye to MacLaren and Hobbs, walked out of the pavilion and around the boundary of the empty field as the sun set purple and fiery orange in the western sky. By the time he got home to Fairmount the stars were out.

Saturday 18 July 1915

'Gilbert, there's a commotion outside. I think you should come.'

Agnes was calling him from the back door. He left the basket of vegetables he'd picked, brushed the dirt from his hands and walked back to the house. He looked out of a front window and saw a platoon of men in khaki in the lane, lined up and facing the house. Their Colonel was marching towards the door, on which he rapped three times.

Eva opened it and he heard the Colonel ask if Dr Grace was at home.

'It's all right Eva, I'm coming,' he said and made his way to the door.

'Can I help you, Colonel?'

'Dr Grace. Please forgive the intrusion: Colonel Tamplin of the Veteran Athletes' Corp. These are some of my men. We are all sportsmen. We are moving from Blackheath to Chislehurst and I couldn't help noticing that the route brought us past your door. I hope you don't mind, sir, but the men and I would like to send you our greetings and best wishes on the occasion of your sixty-seventh birthday today.'

'That's very kind of you, Colonel, very kind of you indeed. I am honoured.'

The Colonel turned to the soldiers lined up to attention in the lane and Grace stepped outside the door on to the drive.

'Company,' called the Colonel. 'Three cheers for Doctor Grace on the occasion of his birthday. Hip, hip.'

'Hooray!'

'Hip, hip.'

'Hooray!'

'Hip, hip.'

'Hooray!'

The Colonel turned and saluted the Old Man, who took two steps forward and addressed them all.

'Gentlemen,' he began, 'I beg to thank you for the honour you have done me. I never saw finer soldiers than I have seen here today and I hope to see as good wherever I go. I wish you all the best and a safe return from your service to your families.'

He shook the Colonel's hand, turned and bowed slightly to the men, and watched as the Colonel marched back to the lane and led them off up the hill towards Chislehurst.

Once the sound of marching boots on the road had died away, he went back through the house and returned to his vegetables.

Monday 7 September 1915

It was late in the evening and he was catching up with some correspondence. The room was dark save for the vulcan glow of the last coals in the grate and the pool of light spilled on to his desk by the lamp. It lit his scratching pen, the embossed notepaper, the cricket ball that he threw from hand to hand whenever he was sitting there thinking. It lit his ink pot and blotter. It lit the thick corkscrew hairs of his beard and the cheeks, nose and forehead made leathery by decades of outdoor activity. It lit the thin strands of grey hair falling forward as he wrote and it was caught in the brightness of his eyes. The clock on the mantelpiece struck 11.30.

That aside, the only sounds were the scratching of his pen and the quiet rush of air into his nostrils. He didn't notice the faint booms from the direction of Millwall Docks: they were too distant, barely carried by the breeze from the north-west. His pen scratched on.

Further north, Hauptmann Richard von Wobeser's SL.2 Zeppelin crossed the Thames to Bermondsey and turned east, ready to unload bombs on Greenwich. Four were dropped close together, the sound of the explosions carried south-east, the edges smoothed off them as they spread until by the time they reached

Mottingham they were faint, barely tangible, low rumbles, like distant thunder.

His pen ceased its scratching and he looked up from the paper, his glance darting from side to side. Seconds later another faint boom, then another, then two more as a total of four bombs landed in Greenwich Park. Alarm flashed across his face. His pen dropped on to the table.

He heaved himself out of his chair, made his way through the house to the back door, opened it and listened. Four more rumbles, further distant now as the SL.2 headed further east to Charlton and on to Woolwich.

His breath became quicker, his mouth dry. The booms had stopped. It was three weeks since the last Zeppelin raid on London. He hadn't heard that one, it was too far north, as was the first one back in May that hit Stoke Newington, but he'd heard about them. These explosions tonight, they must be Zeppelins, too. They were closer than before, he could hear them. They were in the distance but he could hear them. The previous raids had killed people, in their homes. Every boom he'd just heard, each one could have killed people.

The war bothered him enough when reading about events on the Western Front in the newspapers. Sometimes he avoided the papers altogether, sometimes he read every word (the naval reports were the hardest, knowing Edgar was out there somewhere in the maritime front line). But at least it was still all somewhere else. These confounded Zeppelins brought the war to London, to the streets, the pubs, the factories, shops and offices. They came on the breeze, these giant machines of doom against which the English Channel, Britain's ultimate defence, was no barrier any more.

He stood and listened for a few minutes but heard nothing more. He made his way back to his office, picked up the pen and tried to finish the letter he was writing but the words wouldn't come. His mind was taxed now and the light from the lamp illuminated the fear in his eyes. He threw down the pen, stood up sharply from the chair and began to pace up and down the room, his thoughts disordered, his heart racing, his breath short.

He was still pacing 20 minutes later when suddenly he stopped. What was that? He tilted his head to one side in an effort to hear it better. In the distance, somewhere out there in the night, there was a faint, low hum. As he listened he could hear it growing gradually louder. He didn't know it but what he could hear was the LZ.74 Zeppelin commanded by Hauptmann Friedrich George, heading south. He'd crossed the coast at Clacton some two hours earlier and made his way to London, unloading bombs on Cheshunt. He'd passed directly over the Tower of London just after midnight and used up all the rest of his payload over Bermondsey,

Rotherhithe and Deptford. Now he was heading home, skirting around south-east London in a wide arc that passed over Bromley and was now heading for Chislehurst, meaning the LZ.74 would fly close to the home of W.G. Grace, the great cricketer.

Somewhere in the darkness a couple of thousand feet below, the Old Man was listening to the humming growing louder and looking up at the ceiling as if his eyes could bore through the plaster and brick and slate and locate the rumbling demon of the skies from where he stood.

He hurried to the garden again, flinging open the back door, running out to the middle of the lawn and staring up at the sky. It was another clear night and somewhere between him and that canopy of stars there was mortal, evil danger. The noise had grown louder now, not overhead but still loud enough for a few lamps to go on in bedrooms along Mottingham Lane. He turned his head from side to side in an attempt to locate the source of the sound but it seemed to come from everywhere, from all directions at once. His breath was coming in short gasps and his eyes flashed in the night, his fear mixing with a rising anger. He wanted to run towards the noise as much as he wanted to run from it but all he could do was stand and stare at the sky. The throbbing hum grew louder now; the machine must be getting closer. He could almost feel the vibrations in his chest.

Somewhere in the sky Hauptmann George lowered his binoculars, looked at his map and told his navigator to straighten the course and head north-east for the coast of Essex. It had been a successful night in which stealth had won again. He was justifiably pleased with himself and sat down at a table, put the binoculars to one side and opened the ship's log to update his report.

As his pen scratched over the paper he could not have known that somewhere in the darkness below there was a frightened old man with a long, grey beard looking up at the night sky, shaking his fist and bellowing, 'You devils! You devils!' in the direction of an invisible leviathan sailing serenely on through the heavens.

Friday 9 October 1915

It was one of those autumn days washed in golden light from a sun that barely rises above the treetops. The Old Man's shadow was long as he scraped the two wooden-handled boards together and lifted some more crisp, ochre leaves from the putting green to place them in the wheelbarrow. He stopped, took off his hat, wiped his sleeve across his brow, balled his fist against his hip and breathed out heavily. He'd never liked autumn: it had always meant the end of the cricket season. In the garden it also seemed to be about decay: the dead leaves, the rotting wind-fallen apples, the skeletal branches of the trees and bushes.

Today, though, he looked upon it differently. The colours seemed more intense than he'd ever seen: the golds, the browns and the pale blue of the sky. The air had a heady musk to it, woody with a hint of smoke: it smelt of work finished and labour done.

He was nearly done for the day himself. There wasn't too much to do in the garden at this time of year, just keeping the place tidy. He looked at the sky: he'd fancied getting in an hour's putting practice before the day was out but the long shadows told him it would be dark before long.

The thought of work finished made him think of John Dann's funeral earlier in the summer. The genial Irish clergyman had been his brother-in-law, married to his sister Lizzy, but he'd passed away in July. The Old Man had travelled down to Downend church for the funeral with Agnes and his brother Alfred and after the service the congregation had gathered at the graveside and sung 'Now The Labourer's Task Is O'er'.

He picked up the handles of the wooden barrow and began wheeling it towards the end of the garden. The wheel squeaked and its cargo of leaves shifted and jumped with the jolts and hummocks of the garden before he tipped them into the pile he was preparing for the bonfire. But that was for another day.

He turned and pushed the barrow back towards the house, singing softly to himself.

'Now the labourer's task is o'er; now the battle day is past …'

He noticed that the squeak in the wheel had stopped.

'Now upon the farther shore …'

He noticed that he couldn't hear himself singing.

'… Lands the voyager at l—'

He noticed that he couldn't hear anything at all. His right arm swung out and the back of his hand smacked against the trunk of a tree. He tried to control it, to place his hand against the tree for support but it wasn't there. The right side of his head felt strange as if his hat was being pulled hard down over his eye but his hat was over there on the putting green. The right side of his body went numb and he could feel himself falling but it was a slow descent, almost as if it were a dream. He was lying on his side now, looking up towards the house. His cheek should feel cold against the ground, he thought, but he couldn't feel anything.

Then, as if in slow motion, he saw Agnes appearing framed in the doorway. She picked up her skirts and moved towards him. He knew she was running but she was moving so slowly. Everything was moving slowly, a bird overhead, how did it stay in the air and move so slowly?

Agnes drew nearer and he could see her mouth moving and knew she was calling to him. He wanted to respond and tell her he was all right, everything was all right, but he couldn't. Out of the silence her voice came, muffled, she'd nearly reached him now, and he could just make out what it was she was saying.

'Gilbert! Gilbert!'

Tuesday 13 October 1915

'ILLNESS OF DR W.G. GRACE – The cricket world will regret to learn, by the authority of a Bristol correspondent, that news has reached Dr. W.G. Grace's friends at Bristol that a few days ago the veteran cricketer had a seizure which has affected his speech. He is receiving every possible attention at his residence in Kent, and the latest information is to the effect that the "Grand Old Man's" condition shows signs of improvement.' *Birmingham Daily Mail*

Wednesday 14 October

Wednesday 14 October 1915

'They came again last night, Shrimp.'

His speech was still a little slurred but nothing like the first 24 hours when he could barely make a sound.

'Who did, Doctor?' asked Henry Leveson Gower, one of a trickle of visitors who had called in on the Old Man since news of his illness had spread through his cricketing network.

'The Zeppelins, man! The Hun!'

He'd been confined to his bed since the stroke. The doctors agreed that all being well he should make a full recovery, although his speech might not return exactly to how it was, but it could be a slow process and he should rest as much possible for the time being. He'd never in his life spent as much time in bed and was immensely frustrated at being unable to burn off any of the energy that still coursed through him even while incapacitated.

He'd heard them, the invisible devils that come in the night with their humming engines to drop fire and death upon the innocent. He was dozing when the hum first appeared on the fringes of his consciousness and it jolted him awake. His legs wouldn't obey him and refused to move so he lay there, eyes flashing and darting, not being able to tell how many there were, how near they were, whether they were coming closer or moving away. He'd roared with frustration and fear and brought Agnes running in, her face as white as her nightdress, asking, Gilbert, what on earth's the matter, trying to soothe him.

He wouldn't settle. He felt even more defenceless than before, even more frustrated and angry, even more frightened by these monstrous machines that rained death upon the country. What kind of brute could do such a thing? Army fighting army, that was one thing, that was war, but dropping bombs indiscriminately on civilians, on women and children? The mix of anger and fear ate away at him and he'd lain awake all night fretting and pondering, straining his ears for the terrifying portent of that low hum of engines until the first fringes of dawn seeped around the edges of the curtains and he fell into a doze, dreaming of bombs and flames.

'Ah yes, I heard they were over last night,' said Leveson Gower. 'The West End, apparently, as people were leaving the theatres. Monstrous. Just monstrous.'

'I can't get them out of my head, Harry,' said Grace. 'Sometimes I can hear them even when I know they're not up there.'

It surprised his visitor to hear the Champion like this. He had always been such a colossus that it felt wrong to see him so vulnerable, so clearly distressed by the Zeppelin raids. It was barely five months since the Red Cross game at Catford where, even though he wasn't in the best of health, he was still that huge presence, as if he was carrying cricket itself on those broad shoulders and it was no trouble to him at all.

He barely recognised the gaunt figure in the bed, haunted, pale and frightened. The air raids were the talk of London but nobody seemed as perturbed by them as the old man in the bed in front of him. For nearly all his life the only things in the sky had been the clouds, the birds and the occasional cricket ball: these giant flying machines must have seemed to him like something from another world altogether.

'Come now, Doctor,' he said, 'a few airships? Think of the demon bowlers you've faced over the years, and on some interesting wickets, too. You once had Jones put a ball clean through your beard and didn't flinch!'

Grace turned to him and tried to prop himself up on an elbow.

'The difference is, Shrimp, that I could *see* those buggers. I can't see these.'

On his way out, Leveson Gower spoke to Agnes as she helped him with his coat.

'He is very disturbed by the raids,' she said. 'Mr Ashley-Cooper had sent him the proofs of his biography of E.M. to check and that seems to take his mind off them for a while, but he tires easily and has to put them down, and when he's alone with his thoughts he becomes so anxious again.'

Leveson Gower asked Agnes to keep him informed of the Old Man's condition, put on his hat and headed out into the drizzle. Agnes closed the door behind him, turned, and looked up the stairs.

Saturday 23 October 1915

He woke, breathed deeply, rubbed an eye but didn't feel any different. He kept his eyes closed, sensing it was very early. His hip ached from the fall he'd had a couple of days earlier when he'd tried to get out of bed and his legs had buckled beneath him. How Agnes had scolded him for that and how he regretted growing angry at her. It was born out of frustration, nothing else: it wasn't the pain, it was having to come to terms with the fact that his body wouldn't do what he told it to do any more.

His eyes flickered open to darkness. He had no idea of the time but there didn't appear to be anyone else moving in the house. His limbs felt heavy so he'd lay there until the clock struck and told him the time.

There was a tightness in his chest, as if a weight lay upon it: probably the heavy eiderdown on which Agnes insisted. She said it was to keep him warm on these cold autumn nights but he suspected it was because she thought it would help keep him from trying to get out of bed again.

The clock over the fireplace whirred into action.

Ding … ding … ding … ding … ding.

Five o'clock. Very early. He'd had a fitful night: his hip ached and he'd had frantic dreams, none of which he could remember. He wished he was awake this early in order to run with the hounds, or go and have a net in the garden. No nets until spring now. Blast it.

The eiderdown seemed to be getting heavier somehow; he must have a word with Agnes and promise her that he wouldn't try to get out of bed unaided again if she'd only take the infernal thing away. He couldn't move under it at all now. He turned his head towards the window and looked at the stars. It took a second to realise that the curtains were closed so he shouldn't have been able to see them, yet there they were, more beautiful than ever. He remembered the time he'd seen one pulsing with light and smiled at how he'd said goodnight to Bessie.

And then they were in the room with him, all around him. Stars behind stars, as if they were surrounding him. And there was Bessie's star, hanging over the end of the bed, growing brighter with a pulse, almost beating like a heart. He tried to move, to have a better look, and found that although he couldn't seem to his limbs no longer felt heavy; rather, they were weightless. His hip had stopped hurting and the weight had lifted from his chest now, too. What a relief. The stars seemed to be all round him now. How could that be? Bessie's star seemed to be drawing closer to him, or maybe the star was drawing him towards it, he couldn't be sure. He had an urge to close his eyes and did so for a brief moment, but when he opened them the sun was out and it was dazzling him.

His eyes adjusted to the light and he became aware of a woman's form in front of him, in a long skirt and a halterneck blouse. He tried to adjust to the glare.

'Agnes?' he said.

There was a girlish giggle, one full of joy, like a stream over stones. One he recognised. His eyes adjusted further to the light.

'Bessie! My Bessie!'

She smiled back at him, and he noticed she was standing by a low, white gate and beyond the gate was the most exquisitely manicured turf. She opened the gate and smiled, inclining her head to indicate he should go through. He adjusted his pads, felt the weight of the bat in his hand and took a step forward. The sun was still very bright in his eyes, it might take a while for them to adjust once he got to the wicket. At the moment he couldn't even see the field much beyond the gate, so dazzling was the light. He pulled his battered old MCC cap down as far as he could and, peering from what little shade remained under its mashed peak, looked at Bessie, still smiling, still holding the gate open for him.

He was ready to go out there, ready to play everything on its merits. He walked down the shallow steps, smiled back at Bessie as he passed her and strode confidently through the gate, on to the grass and into the brilliant light, safe and happy in the knowledge that the moment was upon him.

'DEATH OF DR W.G. GRACE – GRAND OLD MAN OF CRICKET – We regret to announce that Dr. W.G. Grace, the famous cricketer, died this morning from sudden heart failure at his residence, Fairmount, Mottingham, Kent. It was reported that he had had a slight cerebral attack recently, which affected his speech, but yesterday he was reported to be doing well. William Gilbert Grace, affectionately termed the Grand Old Man, was undoubtedly the greatest player cricket has known. It might also be said of him that he founded an empire, the empire of cricket, and there is not the slightest doubt that cricket – England's national game – has played a great part in forming the character of the individual, and therefore of the nation.' *Evening Despatch*

ACKNOWLEDGEMENTS

Thanks to Charlotte Atyeo, Lizzy Kremer, Jane Lawes and of course Jude, the most newlywed of cricket widows.